Depression: A Silent Culprit in Health and Disease

Editors

Puneetpal Singh, PhD

Human Genetics
Punjabi University
Patiala
India

&

Sarabjit Mastana, PhD

Genomics Lab.
Sport
Exercise and Health Sciences
Loughborough University
UK

DEDICATION

DEDICATED TO THE GOD ALMIGHTY WHOSE BLESSINGS WHEN I RECEIVE ARE THE BEST AND BRIM FULL

CONTENTS

PREFACE

This book is about depression, a malady which has tethered to almost every disease condition and metastasized in every section and every phase of life. It discriminates none, remains silent but in due course of time, manifests in a very loud manner. Despite the fact that it is associated significantly to some of the dreaded diseases, it is often considered as an artefact of age or of concomitant health problem and usually not considered amenable to intervention by health practitioners and general physicians. In the last couple of years, researchers have heralded various risk factors that can contribute to depression and documented their preventive measures, but every time, it appears that it is more complex than what we know so far.

The present eBook, "Depression: A Silent Culprit in Health and Disease" is aimed to consolidate state of the art knowledge from scholars of high repute who have contributed immensely in the field of depression. This treatise tries to bring comprehensive review of latest technological advances in understanding and diagnosing depression, its genetic causes and concerns along with post-stroke consequences which impinge substantially upon health and disease.

In the first chapter, "Depression: It Matters!" author Ana Maria Sanchez Peralta has familiarized about the neurotransmitters, which are present in central nervous system and serve as chemical messengers that transmit signal across synapse from one neuron to another. Imbalance of these endogenous chemicals triggers depression and extent of their imbalance decides severity of depression. She has elaborately discussed various forms of antidepressants and their adverse effects, withdrawal aftermaths and contraindications. Therapies to treat depression vary according to its presence in different diseases, information given regarding this in the chapter is noteworthy and justifies that it matters.

Apropos to every query submitted, a musical event is organized in the hall of brain, where central nervous system plays melodious concert and millions of neurons dance to perform synchronized ballet. This symphonized answer can be understood by a rhythmic wave named P300, musicality of which has been interrogated in the second chapter by Prakash *et al.* This chapter engrosses the attention that neurophysiological examination of P300 wave can comprehend the different layers of depression and putforth that application of P300 wave in clinical settings has tremendous potential in diagnostic and prognostic modalities in major depressive disorder.

Third chapter emphasizes that many stroke survivors undergo depression which can be exacerbated by advancing age and if remains untreated, may lead to adverse outcomes and even mortality. In order to understand the age specific depression after stroke and its preventive measures, authors have pointed out several molecular and cellular mechanisms that can contribute to it, while ageing. Some screening instruments and therapeutic strategies for post-stroke depression have also been discussed, which help us to control depression, which otherwise has formidable impact after ischemic stroke in ageing brain.

Fourth chapter emerges from the query that whether gene and genome wide association studies precisely infer genetic contributions for the risk of depression in post genomic era. Albeit, this chapter by Singh *et al.* revolves around the genetic, epigenetic and pharmacogenetic concerns of depression, but persuades to realize that the concept of 'Personal Medicine' proposed by scientists, by which every person will be treated according to the genes one carries, appears to be a distant dream.

Gianluca Serafini and co-workers have browsed seventy published research papers to uncover the utility of diffusion tensor imaging techniques for understanding brain white matter abnormalities in relation to pathophysiology of major depressive disorder and suicidal behavior. They have deduced that microstructural white matter abnormalities located in neural circuits are critically involved in emotional processes and mood regulation, which may result in enhanced vulnerability to psychiatric morbidity contributing to functional impairments. This review chapter offers an indepth understanding of the current knowledge and applicability of diffusion tensor imaging techniques in major depression and suicidal ideation.

I am deeply indebted to Ms. Shallu Khullar for her extended help in style editing of the book. I extend my heartfelt gratitude to Mr. Humaira Hashmi, In-charge eBook department and editorial manager publications, Ms. Hira Aftab, Assistant Manager, eBooks Publications Department, Ms. Maria Baig, Manager Publications and especially Mr. Mahmood Alam, Director Publications, Bentham Science Publishers for their kind support, encouragement and help.

Puneetpal Singh
Department of Human Genetics
Punjabi University, Patiala
India

CONTRIBUTORS

Ana-Maria Buga	Department of Psychiatry and Psychotheraphy University of Medicine Rostock, Rostock, Germany; Center of Clinical and Experimental Medicine, University of Medicine and Pharmacy Craiova, Craiova, Romania
Ana María Sánchez Peralta	Granada University of Pharmacy, Department of Food Science and Physical Chemistry, La Cartuja, Granada, Spain
Aurel Popa-Wagner	Department of Psychiatry and Psychotheraphy, Aging & Psychiatric Disorders Group, Rostock University Medical School, Gehlsheimer Straβe 20 D-18147 Rostock, Germany
Badescu M. George	Clinic of Psychiatry, University of Medicine and Pharmacy Craiova, Craiova, Romania
Changanamkandath Rajesh	Department of Biotechnology, Sri Guru Granth Sahib World University, Fatehgarh Sahib -140406, Punjab, India
Gianluca Serafini	Department of Neuroscience, Rehabilitation, Ophthalmology, Genetics, Maternal and Child Health (DINOGMI), Section of Psychiatry, University of Genoa, IRCCS San Martino, Largo Rosanna Benzi 10, 16100, Genoa, Italy
Madalina Filfan	Center of Clinical and Experimental Medicine, University of Medicine and Pharmacy Craiova, Craiova, Romania; Clinic of Psychiatry, University of Medicine and Pharmacy Craiova, Craiova, Romania
Manjit Singh	Department of Biotechnology, Sri Guru Granth Sahib World University, Fatehgarh Sahib-140406, Punjab, India
Mario Amore	Department of Neuroscience, Rehabilitation, Ophthalmology, Genetics, Maternal and Child Health (DINOGMI), Section of Psychiatry, University of Genoa, IRCCS San Martino, Largo Rosanna Benzi 10, 16100, Genoa, Italy
Martino Belvederi Murri	Department of Neuroscience, Rehabilitation, Ophthalmology, Genetics, Maternal and Child Health (DINOGMI), Section of Psychiatry, University of Genoa, IRCCS San Martino, Largo Rosanna Benzi 10, 16100, Genoa, Italy
Matteo Respino	Department of Neuroscience, Rehabilitation, Ophthalmology, Genetics, Maternal and Child Health (DINOGMI), Section of Psychiatry, University of Genoa, IRCCS San Martino, Largo Rosanna Benzi 10, 16100, Genoa, Italy
Priyanka Rastogi	Clinical Psychologist & Free-lance Researcher, Sai Krupa Hospital, Mathikere, Bangalore, 560054, India
Ravi Prakash	Department of Physiology, M.S. Ramaiah Medical College, Mathikere, Bangalore, 560054, India
Srinivasa R.	Department of Neurology, M.S. Ramaiah Medical College, Bangalore, 560054, India

CHAPTER 1

Depression: It Matters!

Ana María Sánchez Peralta*

Granada University of Pharmacy, Department of Food Science and Physical Chemistry, La Cartuja, Granada, Spain

Abstract: It is well documented in the literature that there is high prevalence of depression in various diseases and is also a risk factor for the development of certain diseases, such as cardiovascular disease or diabetes. Depression can delay the convalescence and may have effects on treatment states. Pharmacological treatments for depression are based on increasing activity of neurotransmitters which are normally diminished in this disease. Various intrinsic or extrinsic factors play role for the development of depression. Treatments vary according to the type of depression. Hence, diagnosing the exact cause of depression is very important. The adverse effects of antidepressant drugs on other disease conditions in a depressed patient should be considered, particularly on the central nervous system and the cardiovascular system. The interactions of various antidepressants may cause the "Serotonin Syndrome" by synergy effect. There are also interactions with other drugs at the kinetic level due to the role of cytochrome P450 (CYP450) in the metabolism of antidepressants and many others (drugs or molecules). These interactions can be competitive or non-competitive with a result of agonism (synergies) or antagonism, with the change of relative effects of each one. Because antidepresant effect is at long term, the quick substitution of one antidepressant with other usually gives mixed effects of both and interactions at the beginning. Withdrawal should be gradual otherwise, it may cause discontinuation syndrome. The symptoms of this syndrome should not be confused with the patient's symptoms. The worsening of other ailments and enlargement of convalescence can be diminished with right type of antidepressant treatment.

Keywords: Antidepressants, depression, disease, interactions, risk factor.

INTRODUCTION

Depression is a medical illness accompanied by symptoms of fatigue, sadness, self-limiting attitude, neglect, disability, guilt, *etc.* It can be triggered by certain life events such as childhood neglect, death of a loved one, job problems or other major life changes. Some times medical treatment given for other ailments can lead to depression. It can also happen as a symptom of other illnesses like multiple sclerosis,

***Corresponding author Ana María Sánchez Peralta Granada:** University of Pharmacy, Department of Food Science and Physical Chemistry, La Cartuja, Granada, Spain; Tel: +34952493306; +34637802725; E-mail: anam.sanchez.peralta@gmail.com

Puneetpal Singh and Sarabjit Mastana (Eds)

stroke, chronic pain, cancer, hypothyroidism and so on. Depending upon the trigger, depression can be endogenous which is primarily biological and genetic in nature or exogenous caused by highly stressful situations. Endogenous depression is usually expressed by the state of melancholy with increased risk of suicide. In these cases psychotherapy is less useful and intensive pharmacotherapy with tricyclic antidepressants is the most effective treatment. Exogenous depression often is associated with people having neurotic personality which is manifested by dysthymia, adjustment disorder or reactive depression. In these cases there is a lower risk of suicide. Psychotherapy can be useful along with a range of drugs like selective serotonin reuptake inhibitors (SSRIs) in this case. Biologically, depression is the result of imbalance of chemicals called neurotransmitters with less concentration in many of them. The most studied neurotransmitters involved in depression are serotonin (5-HT), dopamine (DA) and noradrenaline (NA, or even norepinephrine). So the treatment is aimed to increase the effects of these mono-amines. Currently, the mono-amine oxidase inhibitors (MAOIs), tricyclic antidepressants (TCAs or ADT) and selective inhibitor of the reuptake of serotonin (SSRIs), are the pharmacological treatments used currently [1, 2].

CAUSES OF DEPRESSION

Depression has many possible causes including faulty mood regulation by the brain, genetic susceptibility, stressful life events, medications and medical problems. Several of these factors collaborate in the causation of depression. Biologically major cause of depression is low concentration of neurotransmitters (NT), which results in the deficit of neurotransmission, although this does not all cases of depression. The neurotransmitters are endogenous chemicals which are required for the proper functioning of brain and allow transmission of impulses from one neuron to another across synapse. In depression, the interaction of three main neurotransmitters plays role: serotonin, dopamine and epinephrine. The effect of antidepressant is to increase the levels of neurotransmitters thereby enhancing neurotransmission. But the relationship of neurotransmitters is interdependent; for example, serotonin modulates the activity of dopamine and other brain neuromodulators [3, 4].

Serotonin

It is a neurotransmitter found in multiple regions of the central nervous system (Fig. **1**). When present in high levels, causes a sensation of pleasure and wellness, but when present in small quantities it is associated with depressive disorders, anxiety, aggressive states, sleep disorders and mental imbalances. It regulates appetite, balances sexual desire and is involved in controlling body temperature, motor activity and perceptual/cognitive functions. Serotonin is related, along with dopamine and noradrenaline, in processes of distress, anxiety, fear, aggression, as well as eating disorders. It helps in the process of elaboration of melatonin, a protein that is produced in the brain by the pineal gland and is responsible for regulating sleep. It functions as the internal clock of our body and coordinates various biological functions such as body temperature, hormone stress and sleep cycles. Proper coordination of these three elements allows us to have sound sleep. Men tend to sleep more hours because they produce up to 50% more serotonin than women. Throughout the day serotonin levels decrease, so it is necessary to consume foods that help us to produce this neurotransmitter. It is synthesized from the amino acid tryptophan, so that foods rich in this amino acid should be chosen like milk, eggs, turkey, soy, *etc*. Exercise is another option to increase serotonin levels in our body along with meditation, relaxation and yoga as well as sunlight walk, because light favours its levels.

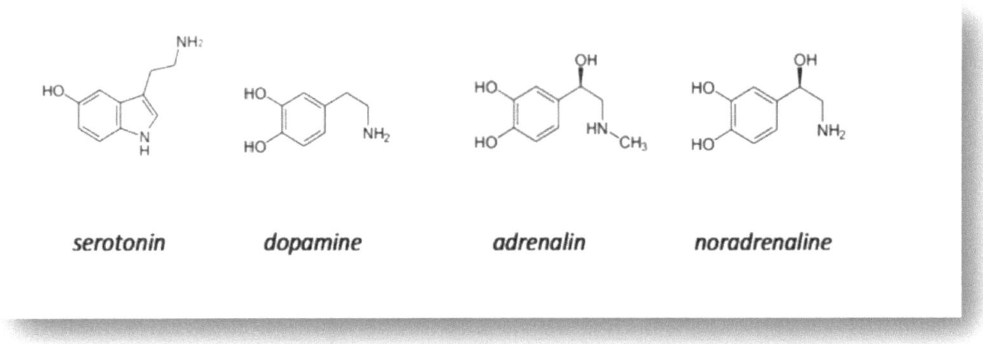

Fig. (1). Neurotransmitters 5-HT, DA, AD and NA.

Dopamine

This hormone and neurotransmitter (neuro-hormone) is a catecholamine (tyrosine derivative) with specific functions in the central nervous system. It is synthesized in the adrenal glands and nervous tissue, released by the hypothalamus where its main function is to inhibit the release of prolactin from the anterior lobe of the pituitary. It is found in large quantities in the substantia nigra. Most of its functions are developed in the brain, regulating important activities such as behaviour, cognition, motor activity, motivation, regulation of milk production, sleep, mood, aspects of attention, and learning. It is known as a neurotransmitter associated with addictions, as hallucinogens or drugs such as cocaine, opium, heroin, snuff and alcohol which activate the dopaminergic system. If dopamine production decreases, decline in endorphins function is also seen. A person in stress will have lower levels of dopamine. Its deficit is related to Parkinson's and muscular non-coordination and its excess with schizophrenia or hallucinations. It is related to pleasure and reward. But dopamine is not only the pleasure molecule as it plays an important role in learning, resulting in more effective memory. It is increased in the infatuation stage because it causes an increase in the activity of brain areas, on the right side, where higher dopamine levels are concentrated which are related to energy and euphoria. Its activity is modulated by serotonin. Foods rich in tyrosine increase dopamine levels like bananas, almonds, apples, watermelons, cherries, yogurt, beans, eggs and meat.

Norepinephrine

Noradrenaline (norepinephrine) is a catecholamine with dual function as a hormone and neurotransmitter. As stress hormone, norepinephrine affects parts of the brain where attention and responding actions are controlled. It stimulates the sympathetic nervous system. Along with adrenaline, noradrenaline is also involved in the "fight-flight" response, preparing to act, directly increasing heart rate, triggering the release of glucose from energy stores and increasing blood flow to the skeletal muscle. Since dopamine is associated with fear and anxiety, it relates to both good and bad memories, prepares for a physical and mental response. Its levels are increased in intense exercise and dangerous situations. It causes oxidation of triglycerides producing fatty acids and glycerol that are liberated into the blood.

Lately less brain-derived neurotrophic factor (BDNF) has been found to be associated with major depression and even considered as a diagnostic marker [4]. BDNF is related to the ability of neuronal plasticity which allows the creation of appropriate connections throughout life, based on learning and positive feelings. Increased BDNF has an antidepressant effect, whereas a decrease in its activity generates depression. Stress increases glucocorticoids, which inhibit the neurotrophic factor, causing depression (in the hippocampus cell is observed greater atrophy and apoptosis). The brain monoamines with their antidepressant effect increase the activity of BDNF [4]. Almost 5% of the general population suffers from depression. About 15-25% of the population suffers from depressive episodes atleast once in their lifetime. Sometimes it masks other diseases such as in iron deficiency- Anemia, which manifests with similar symptoms such as fatigue, tiredness, lack of motivation, apathy or impotence and can lead to a psychiatric medical consultation, although the cause is the deficiency of iron ion (Fe^{++}) [5, 6]. Situations of physical dependence like some chronic disease, post-traumatic stress (accidents, broken hip, surgery) and even diabetes, can also cause the development of depressive illness [6-8].

This means that cause of depressive syndrome can be a direct depression disease itself or the consequence of other illness triggering depressive state. Whatever the state, depression has a negative effect on prognosis of other diseases, can cause worsening and delays improvement. If remains unnoticed, it can lead to suicidal ideation.

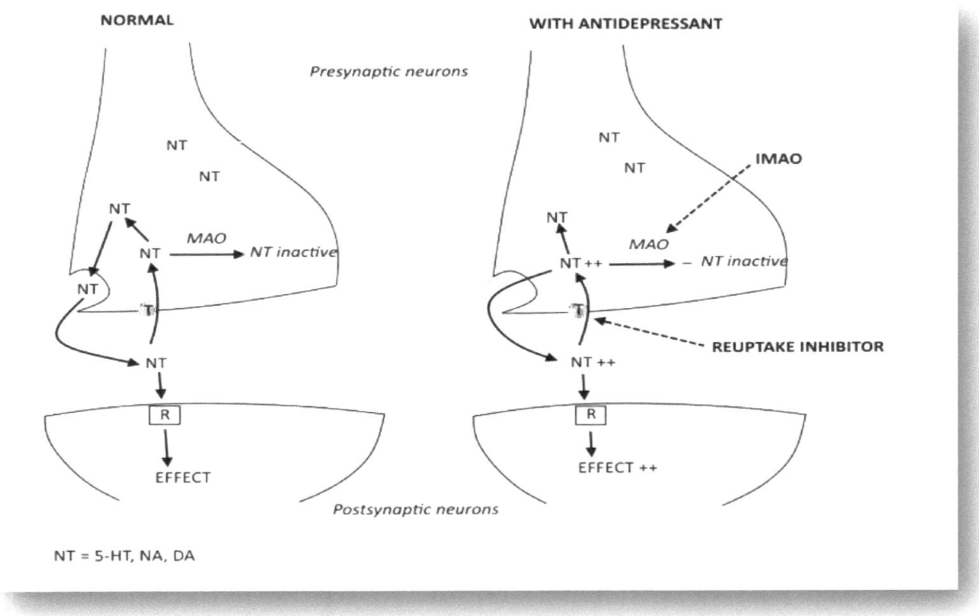

Fig. (2). Activity of antidepressants at the neuronal level.

Depression has not only psychiatric consequences, but has physical impact also by increasing the chances of other major illnesses like coronary heart disease. People with depression have three times higher chances of heart attack. Similarly in type 2 diabetes mellitus, condition worsens as depressed patients do not maintain diet or do exercise. Also it influences immune system in cancer patients or increases inflammatory chemicals in the body. It has been observed that people with signs of depression like feeling of helplessness or impairment suffer more from asthma than the general population. Now a days in hospital care much importance is given to increase the state of optimism in patients to prevent them from going into depressive state which otherwise delays the eventual recovery of the hospitalized patients. If convalescence is shorter the cost of treatment will also decrease [6-10].

TYPES OF DEPRESSION

There are many different types of depression. Before starting treatment, one has to distinguish between endogenous depression where symptoms appear out of nowhere and exogenous depression caused by external reasons (Table **1**). Although both types of depression has significant overlap of symptoms with each other but treatment and care differ to great extent. Since, endogenous depression is caused by genetic or biochemical problems and melancholic personality is riskier on suicide, medications help in dealing with it, and talk or psychotherapy less works; but in exogenous depression, (neurotic personality prevalence), talk therapy or psychotherapy works better, by isolating the life problem that caused the depression. Suicide risk is less in this neurotic personality. If depression persists for two years or longer, it is called persistent depressive disorder. Depression can also accompany some physical illness called somatogenic depression which is further divided into organic depression due to cerebral disorder or depression due to systemic disease [9]. Consumption of drugs like interferon, methyldopa and steroids, toxics and other diseases, may cause iatrogenic depression characteristic of which are asthenia, weakness, drowsiness, laxity and anorexia. Similarly, unipolar depression differs from bipolar depression where in addition to going through low moods, individuals with bipolar disorders have high moods known as mania with possible psychotic symptoms (auditory or visual hallucinations or simple delirium). Although bipolar disorder has a depressive component, the treatment is different. It is with Lithium only or associated with atypical antipsychotics in the maniac phase or with anticonvulsants like valproic acid (VPA). In anxious depressive syndrome or mixed anxiety depressive disorder patients suffer from both anxiety and depressive symptoms [10]. In such cases, treatment becomes difficult as some treatment is effective for depressive state whereas, some is effective for anxiety symptoms. Hence, diagnosing the right type of depression is essential for formulating therapeutic strategy [11-13].

TREATMENTS AND ASSOCIATIONS

Treatment used in depression depends upon the type and severity of the condition. The treatment for severe depression includes antidepressant medications and psychotherapy along with lifestyle changes. As different people have different symptoms and causes of depression so there is no 'one size fits all' treatment of depression. What works for one person might not work for other.

Table 1. Causes and characteristics of different types of depression.

Depression	Endogenous	Exogenous	Secondary
Causes	**Biochemical** prolactin melatonin endogenous cortisol **Genetic** Chromosomal regions of interest: 11pter-p15, 17q11.2, 2q33.34 Genes: APOE, GNB3, MTHFR, SLC6A3, SLC6A4, GxA, among others.	**Psychosocial** Personal problems External conflicts (duel that does not subside in two months) Reactive depression by unexpected problems as disappointments, limiting disease, economic problems, which may be combined with anxiety	**Diseases** Anemia, hypothyroidism, viral infections, cerebral arteriosclerosis **(Drug or Toxic)** **Drugs** steroids, anti-neoplastics, anti-hypertensives (β-propranolol-ACEIs), anti-epileptic (carbamazepine, clonazepam) diuretics(acetazolamide, spironolactone) NSAIDs(indomethacin, metronidazole) **Toxic** alcohol cocaine nicotine
Observations	**Melancholic Personality** (Usually not present prior personality disorders)	**Neurotic personality**	------------
Symptoms	Anorexia, Weight loss Anhedonia, Recurrence, Suicide Risk, Family affective disorders, Seasonal difference(higher in spring and autumn)	Anxiety, Self-pity (psychomotor disorder or delusional ideas)	Adynamia, Asthenia Sleepiness, Laxity, Anorexia

The ultimate aim of the medical practitioner is to look for improvement in mood, standardization of development of daily functions and prevent relapse. In secondary depression, patient should be treated according to the specific causes of the organic condition, *e.g.* in the treatment of anemia, if less iron is the cause of depression, by treatment with this element (Fe^{++}) can cure depression. Many types of antidepressant medications are used, but the drug of choice is SSRI. These are safer and have minor side effects. If there is no effect (which happens in about 50% of cases) this can be associated with a tricyclic antidepressant (TCA) or be changed to another antidepressant of choice (another SSRI or another antidepressant of the second generation). Mono amaine oxidase inhibitors (MAOIs) are prescribed generally when other medications have not worked because of their side effects. Use of these requires strict diet as these interact with cheese, wine *etc*., and have deadly effect [11]. Sometimes a combination of antidepressant is used which can be anti-psychotic or anti-anxiety drug [12].

ANTIDEPRESSANT DRUGS

MAOIs:

- Tranylcypromine (MAOI-AB non-selective, irreversible), prolonged action.
- Moclobemide (MAOI-A selective, reversible), short-acting.

Reuptake inhibitors:

- TCA (tricyclic antidepressants) Block α, H and M receptors, non-selective, so have more safety problems, present a greater number of adverse reactions. These are: Amitriptyline, Clomipramine, Dosulepin, Doxepin, Imipramine, Maprotiline, Nortriptyline, Trimipramine.
- SSRI (selective serotonin reuptake inhibitor) Does not block the M receptors, selected for inhibiting serotonin reuptake, increasing only the effect. Some are: Citalopram, Fluoxetine, Fluvoxamine, Paroxetine, Sertraline.
- NRI (noradrenaline reuptake inhibitor) or (norepinephrine reuptake inhibitor). The NA stays longer doing its effect because of less uptake. These are: Reboxetine.
- SNRI (serotonin-norepinephrine reuptake inhibitor) By inhibiting the reuptake of both neurotransmitters (5-HT and NA) magnify their effects. These are: Duloxetine, Venlafaxine.

- Others: Bupropion (DA and NA), Mianserin (NA and 5-HT) blocking α receptor, Mirtazapine (DA and NA) blocking α and 5-HT receptors, and Trazodone (5-HT) blocking 5-HTreceptor.

Adverse Effects of Antidepressants:

Adverse interactions of reuptake inhibitor antidepressants have been shown in Table **2**.

MAOIs: These have the following side effects:

- Postural hypotension (orthostatic)
- Sedation / Excitement and insomnia
- Weight gain
- Serious interactions with other drugs and foods.

REUPTAKE INHIBITORS: Each of these drugs has one or more side effects as mentioned below:

- Anti-cholinergic effects
- Sedation
- Hypotension
- Cardiac effects
- Sexual inhibition
- Convulsions
- Gastrointestinal effects
- Weight gain

As shown in the table, the TCA may have all these side effects, although gastrointestinal effects are almost nonexisting. Of these, Amitriptyline, clomipramine and doxepin have more pronounced adverse effects than nortriptyline which has fewer side effects. These can cause death by overdose, have cardiovascular effects that lead to sudden death or effects on the central nervous system with confusion, seizures or respiratory depression leading to death.

Table 2. Adverse effects of reuptake inhibitor antidepressants.

Antidepressant Reuptake Inhibitor	Anticholinergic Effects	Sedation	Hypotension	Cardiac Effects	Sexual Inhibi-Tion	Convulsions	Gastrointestinal Effects	Weight Gain
TCA								
Amitriptyline	+++	+++	+++	+++	++	+++	(+)	++
Clomipramine	+++	++	++	+++	+++	+++	+	++
Doxepin	++	+++	+++	+++	++	+++	(+)	++
Imipramine	++	++	++	+++	++	++	(+)	++
Maprotiline	++	++	++	++	++	+	(+)	+
Nortriptyline	+	+	+	++	++	+	(+)	+
Trimipramine	+++	+++	++	+++	++	++	(+)	++
ISRS								
Citalopram		(+)			+++		+++	
Fluoxetine		(+)		(+)	+++	(+)	+++	(+)
Fluvoxamine		(+)			+++		+++	
Paroxetine	(+)	(+)			+++		+++	
Sertraline		(+)			+++		+++	
OTHER								
Bupropion						++++	++	
Mirtazapine		++++	(+)				(+)	(+)
Trazodone		+++		(+)	+		++	+
Venlafaxine				(+)	+++		+++	

SSRIs have lesser adverse effects in general, except gastrointestinal and sexual inhibition, which are even more accentuated than with TCA, but are less dangerous. Consequently SSRIs are safer. Other antidepressants such as bupropion cause seizures only, while mirtazapine causes sedation but has no gastrointestinal side effects. Trazodone presents both sedation and gastrointestinal side effects whereas; venlafaxine presents the gastrointestinal effects and sexual inhibition.

Therefore, while selecting an antidepressant, one should consider these adverse effects for the individual patient according to their potential somatic complaints or symptomatic needs. For example, in case of insomnia, sedation, one of the side effects can play a positive role [3].

Associations Between Different Antidepressants

SSRI + TCA → If no response exists with SSRIs, reduce the dose of TCA.

MAOI + TCA → Contraindicated (unless there is resistance to other treatments)

SSRI + MAOI→ Contraindicated and hence, not advisable.

Serotonin Syndrome

Serotonin is a chemical which helps as a messenger of neuronal activities or enables brain cells to communicate with each other (Fig. **2**). When serotonin levels are less in brain, it is considered to cause depression but, if higher levels of serotonin are released because of some drugs, then it may lead to excessive nerve cell activity that may lead to collection of some deadly manifestations known as serotonin syndrome.

Serotonin syndrome symptoms includes confusion, agitation or restlessness, dilated pupils, changes in body temperature or blood pressure, headache, nausea and/or vomiting, diarrhea, increased heart rate, tremor, loss of muscle coordination, shivering and goose bumps, heavy sweating. In severe cases, serotonin syndrome can be life-threatening. If patient experiences symptoms like high fever, seizures, irregular heartbeat and unconsciousness, then immediately medical help is required. It may be triggered by the association of MAOI with a TCA or SSRI by synergy. MAOIs + TCAs or SSRIs or MAOIs +TCAs or SSRIs. These associations may provoke serotonin syndrome (Fig. **3**). The MAOI enzymes (monoamino oxidases) catalyze the degradation reaction of amine neurotransmitters, including serotonin, dopamine and noradrenaline and inactivate them. These enzymes of the CNS are in the mitochondrial membrane of almost all human cells. Its two types are, MAO-A and MAO-B and both are found in the CNS, neurons and astroglia. Outside the CNS, MAO-A is present in liver, gastrointestinal tract and the placenta. MAO-B is found mainly in the blood and platelets. MAO catalyzes the degradation of neurotransmitters favouring inactivation thereof, so its inhibition (MAOIs effect) favors activated NT permanence arranged to be in the synaptic gap. If diminished synaptic serotonin reuptake is maintained with an inhibitor such as an SSRI or a TCA, then it greatly increases the concentration and effects of serotonin in the synaptic space as reuptake modulates exposure time of neurotransmitters in the receptors. This increased activity of serotonin receptors causes functional disorders as mental changes (agitation, confusion, fixation or mania), autonomic dysfunction (sweating, diarrhea, fever and shivers), neuromuscular disorders (hyperreflexia, incoordination, tremors), seizures, coma and death. Therefore, MAOI + TCA→ Risk of serotonin syndrome, contraindicated or under control. MAOI + SSRI→ Risk of serotonin syndrome, contraindicated and not allowed.

Dopamine is degraded by MAO-A and MAO-B; serotonin, norepinephrine (noradrenaline) and epinephrine (adrenaline) are mostly degraded by MAO-A; (phenyl-ethylamine (FEA) is degraded by MAO-B). Other interactions of antidepressants that can cause serotonin syndrome are: Tryptophan + Lithium, Hypericum + Tramadol, Cocaine + Amphetamines, Triptans + Buspirone. In case of serotonin syndrome, these drugs must be stop given and measures are taken to include serotoninergic antagonists.

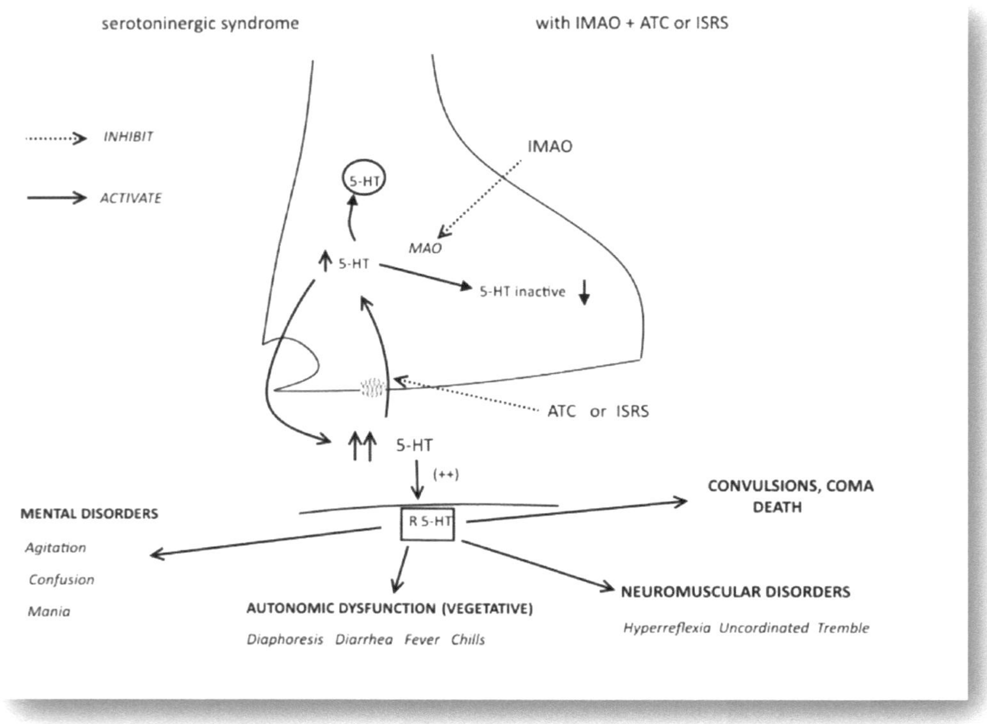

Fig. (3). Serotoninergic syndrome by interaction of IMAO with TCA or ISRS.

Synergisms and Antagonisms

Synergism is defined as a joint action of two drugs in such a manner that one supplements or enhances the action of the other to produce an affect greater than that which may be obtained with either one of the drugs in equivalent quantity or produce effects that could not be obtained with any safe quantity of either drug or both.

Antagonism is defined as the opposing actions of drugs. Because cytochrome P450 and the large number of isoforms of P450 isoenzymes (CYP) affecting the metabolism of antidepressants and other drugs, such as CYP1A2, CYP2C9, CYP2C19, CYP2D6, CYP3A4 cytochromes, there are many possible pharmacokinetic interactions that increase or decrease the effect of antidepressant when combined with these drugs. If the antidepressant and the drug that interacts with it, are substrates of the same CYP, it has a competitive enzyme inhibition, being able to give greater or lesser effect of each drug. We can also have a non-competitive enzyme inhibition, being one substrate of the CYP and the other inhibitor of it, decreasing the metabolism of antidepressants and increasing its effectiveness. You can also give both, being the same CYP substrates and inhibitors of other CYP, which competitively and non-competitively will increase or decrease the effects of each drug.

In a CYP enzyme induction, the inducer drug increases the rate of metabolism of the antidepressant decreasing its effect. They are inducers of CYP1A2 enzyme that metabolizes TCAs (amitriptyline, clomipramine and imipramine), barbiturates, phenytoin and smoke snuff, thus decreasing its effect. This enzyme is inhibited by other antidepressants of family of SSRIs such as fluoxetine or fluvoxamine that increase the effect of the TCA. Other inhibitors of this enzyme are cimetidine, fluoroquinolones, rofecoxib and tacrine. They are inducers of CYP2C9 enzyme, the rifampicin and inhibitors of areamiodarone, azole antifungals and SSRI fluoxetine and fluvoxamine. CYP2C19 inhibitors are fluvoxamine, omeprazole and valdecoxib. CYP2D6 inducers are rifampicin. Inhibitors are bupropicn, cimetidine, dextropropoxyphene, propafenone and SSRI fluoxetine, paroxetine and sertraline.

They are inducers of CYP3A4 carbamazepine, dexamethasone, phenytoin, phenobarbital, Hypericum and rifampicin. Inhibitors are azole antifungals, cimetidine, fluoxetine, macrolides, verapamil and grapefruit juice. In their interactions, one must consider that other drugs are also substrates of the different CYP isoenzymes, influencing their activity in accordance to be more or less linked.

Other drugs substrates of CYP1A2: caffeine, clozapine, duloxetine, flecainide, theophylline, triptans, Warfarin. Other substrates of CYP2C9 are coxibs, diclofenac, statins, phenytoin, sulfonylureas, Warfarin. Other substrates of CYP2C19 are diazepam, citalopram, phenytoin, imipramine, moclobemide. Other substrates of CYP2D6 are the β-blocker carvedilol, metoprolol and propranolol,

TCAs imipramine, nortriptyline and trimipramine, antipsychotics clozapine and risperidone, and other drugs such as duloxetine, mirtazapine, opioids, paroxetine, propafenone, trazodone and venlafaxine. Other CYP3A4 substrates are the TCAs-amitriptyline and imipramine, and antihistamines, azole antifungals, anti-neoplastics, benzodiazepines (alprazolam, midazolam, triazolam), blockers of calcium channels, buspirone, carbamazepine, cyclosporine, statins, estrogen, protease inhibitors, opioids, propafenone, reboxetine, zolpidem [3, 13, 14].

Because of these interactions practical cases of known interactions can be explained.

Medical Interactions

TCA

1) H2 receptor antagonists is the antiacid effect example, by inhibiting CYP1A2, CYP2D6 and CYP3A4 as well as other drugs (bupropion, duloxetine, fluoxetine, fluvoxamine, paroxetine, sertraline), make these CYPs not metabolized TCA into inactive metabolites, so these TCA activity is increased by increasing its concentration in plasma, and anticholinergic adverse effects are therefore larger. If it is also associated with an old antipsychotic like chlorpromazine that further increase these anticholinergic adverse effects, it can lead to heat stroke, intestinal stasis and atropinic psychosis. One must reduce the antidepressant in this case but not increase the antipsychotic. One should replace cimetidine for famotidine or ranitidine.

2) With alcohol the gastric emptying, is slower which increases the absorption of TCA. It also gives CYP inhibition with lesser metabolism to inactive products and the effect of CNS depression is multiplied. Motor skills and learning ability are affected. Patient should not consume alcohol in the first two weeks of treatment which can improve its adaptation with TCA.

3) With antiepileptics such as carbamazepine, CYP3A4 activity is increased by increasing the inactivation of imipramine into inactive metabolites and reducing the antidepressant effect. The same thing happens to amitriptyline, citalopram, doxepin, nortriptyline or sertraline. Phenytoin and barbiturates also increase the activity of CYP3A4 by lowering the concentration of active antidepressant in blood. Besides this, TCA

decreases the seizure threshold. The association of barbiturate and TCA can also lead to respiratory depression.

SSRI

1) With benzodiazepines, such as alprazolam, bromazepam, diazepam, nitrazepam, midazolam or triazolam that are used as anxiolytics, the SSRIs such as fluvoxamine or fluoxetine lead to increased benzodiazepine effects by inhibiting CYP3A4 that metabolizes them. So inactive metabolites decrease, increasing the effect of benzodiazepine. Adverse effects of benzodiazepines are also increased, such as sedation, dizzyness, unsteadyness and decreased concentration. The doses of benzodiazepines should be reduced or substituted by lorazepam, lormetazepam, oxazepam and temazepam. Fluoxetine can also be substituted with sertraline.

2) With NSAIDs, SSRIs increase the risk of bleeding, as serotonin reuptake is inhibited on the platelet leading to lower platelet aggregation. NSAIDs by inhibiting the COX-1 cause less gastroprotective prostaglandins. Trazodone also acts on the 5-HT_{2A} inhibiting them and decreasing platelet aggregation. So any association of SSRIs with NSAID can lead to gastroduodenal bleeding. While taking these antidepressants, paracetamol should be used or NSAIDs be replaced with ibuprofen. SSRIs can also be replaced by nortripilina (TCA) or reboxetine (NRI). Gastric protective prophylaxis can be established with misoprostol or omeprazole.

3) With warfarin, fluvoxamine (SSRI) inhibits its metabolism by inhibiting CYP1A2, CYP2C19 and even CYP2C9 that transform warfarin into its inactive metabolites. Therefore, warfarin is increased in blood which increases the risk of bleeding. Fluvoxamine, like other SSRIs, inhibits the 5-HT receptors of platelets, decreasing platelet aggregation. Therefore, caution must be taken while using SSRIs with everything that can increase bleeding.

4) With new antipsychotics such as clozapine or risperidone, CYP1A2 is inhibited and degrades these to inactive metabolites thereby increasing the antipsychotics concentration in plasma and their adverse effects. Clozapine in higher concentrations can cause sedation, anticholinergic symptoms and seizures. Risperidone in greater concentration causes

extrapyramidal symptoms and gynecomastia. The same effect of inhibition of CYP1A2 is produced by fluoxetine, sertraline and even citalopram [3, 13, 18].

5) Secondary effects like Arrhythmias are seen in the following interactions:

- Fluoxetine, paroxetine or fluvoxamine with tricyclic antidepressants cause arrhythmia, seizures and coma.
- Fluvoxamine with cisapride cause arrhythmias and prolongation of QT interval heart.
- Fluvoxamine with theophylline cause arrhythmias and seizures.

6) Other effects observed in interaction of different medicines:

- Fluoxetine, fluvoxamineor paroxetine with antiepileptic like carbamazepine or phenytoin cause cerebellar dysfunction and neurotoxicity.
- Fluoxetine or bupropion with paroxetine causes seizures.
- Propranolol or metoprolol with fluoxetine or fluvoxamine enhances toxicity of the β-blocker, but does not occur with other β-blockers.
- Cyproheptadine (antihistamine), with fluoxetine or paroxetine inhibits the effect of antidepressants.
- Clarithromycin (macrolide) with fluoxetine enhances its toxicity, so another macrolide should be used.
- Hypericum powers SSRI toxicity.
- Itraconazole (oral antifungal) enhances the toxicity of fluoxetine.
- Fluoxetine can suppress the analgesic effect of morphine (opioid).
- Sumatriptan (antimigraine) with fluoxetine, inhibit the sumatriptan effect [2, 12].

DEPRESSED STATE IN OTHER DISORDERS

1. Bipolar Disorder

Lithium treatment is the first choice in this disorder. If the depressive phase is mild, it can be treated with the same lithium or with lamotrigine having antidepressant effect or with an SSRI [15].

2. Alzheimers Disease

The depressive and anxiety symptoms coexist with other psychopathological processes, organic disease and dementia. In these patients it is sometimes difficult to detect depression because of their intellectual disabilities, but can be confirmed when there is an improvement in mood after an antidepressant treatment. It seems that the dual action of SNRIs on serotonin and norepinephrine, like venlafaxine, is most suitable [16].

3. Atypical Depression

It involves symptoms like weight gain, increased appetite, excessive sleep, fatigue or extreme sensitivity to rejection. MAOIs are recommended in these cases [17].

4. Puerperal Depression

It appears in postpartum period. For treatment, TCAs are found more suitable than SSRIs. These should be considered if lactation is going on [18].

5. Premenstrual Dysphoric Disorder

These are depressive symptoms which occur in women due to hormonal changes prior to menstruation period. Generally there are natural or behavioral treatments such as cognitive behavioral therapy (CBT), increase in vitamins B, exercise and psychotherapy. In case an antidepressant is to be used then SSRIs are the first choice [19].

6. Dysthymic Disorder

It is associated with neurotic depression where people are chronically sad or depressed. In them both group therapy and psychotherapy along with antidepressants of SSRI group are useful although, the chronicity and possible long-term needs should be considered [20].

7. Adaptive Disorder or Reactive Depression

In this type of depression symptoms arise in response to a stress reaction (disappointment, economic problems, *etc.*) with a result of depressed or mixed mood, combined with depression and anxiety. Many depressions are actually adjustment disorders, after an adverse event. Psychotherapy and treatment with an SSRI is useful in such cases [21].

8. Unspecified Depressive Disorder or Anxiety-Depressive Syndrome

In this patients suffer from both anxiety and depressive symptoms of limited or equal intensity. Such patients are given SSRIs at the first place as a pharmacological treatment. Some studies have endorsed the possibility of cognitive behavioral therapy as the only treatment, with the improvement in quality of life. The therapist should make an effort not to treat a male or female patient differently [22].

9. Reaction of Duel (Grief)

Symptoms of major depression can occur after the death of a loved one, which may lessen over time. But if it takes more than two months with marked functional impairment, it should be diagnosed as major depression liable for treatment. SSRIs should be the first choice but associated problems like anxiety or insomnia should also be considered [23].

10. Depression in Elderly

It is usually masked by effects of other problems like loss of appetite, insomnia, loss of interest, hypochondriacal thoughts, anxiety or irritability. Often depression in the elderly has been taken as prelude to dementia. The effective treatment is psychotherapy and use of antidepressants of latest generation (SSRIs, ISSN, *etc.*), usually at lower doses keeping into consideration other medicines given for various disease conditions like blood thinners or other psychoactive drugs [24].

11. Depression in Childhood and Adolescence

Its diagnosis may be difficult because normal behaviour varies from one childhood stage to another. The symptoms can be an irritant-defiant behaviour, conduct of parasuicide, taking drugs, anxiety or learning disorder. It may begin in early childhood with diffuse somatic complaints, eating disorders, enuresis and boredom. Usually, there is family history. In such cases, psychotherapy, behavioral therapy and SSRI antidepressants are often helpful, with noticeable changes in attitude. Fluoxetine is the first choice but sertraline and citalopram are also given [25].

Withdrawal of Antidepressant

Rapid withdrawal of antidepressant has adverse effects and causes a number of symptoms. These effects are named "Interdose Discontinuation Symptoms" or IDS. Discontinuation syndromes are in part related to drugs with shorter half-lives like venlafaxine which has a short half-life of 6 hours and have been clinically reported. These symptoms are also found with the use of paroxetine which has a longer half-life of 21- 24 hours [26, 27].

The symptoms of discontinuation syndrome are:

1. Balance disorders (lightheadedness, dizziness, ataxia, *etc.*)
2. Gastrointestinal symptoms (nausea, vomiting, diarrhea, *etc.*)
3. Flu-like symptoms (fatigue, lethargy, myalgia, chills, rhinorrhea, headache, *etc.*)
4. Sensory disturbances (paresthesias, electric shock sensation, unpleasant sensations in the occipital region, *etc.*)
5. Sleep disturbances (excessive and often terrifying dreams, insomnia, somnolence, *etc.*)
6. Other psychological symptoms are anxiety, agitation, crying spells and irritability.

Apart from these, other behavioural symptoms have also been described like hyperactivity, depersonalization, decreased mood, amnesia, confusion, decreased concentration, slowed thinking and even severe behavioral disorders such as aggressiveness and impulsivity (suicidal and homicidal thoughts, shoplifting, *etc.*). These symptoms should not be confused with side effects of antidepressants or medical interactions or with patient's own symptoms. Withdrawal should be as slow and gradual as possible, especially in venlafaxine and paroxetine. Even after gradual withdrawal venlafaxine can still exhibit IDS.

Other Prescriptions for Antidepressants

Fluvoxamine is used in obsessive-compulsive disorder (OCD) and is the first SSRI approved for use in children. It is presecribed for OCD in adults, adolescents and children. It has also been used for the treatment of post traumatic stress disorder (PTSD), obesity, bulimia nervosa, schizophrenia, panic disorder, social anxiety disorder and autism.

TCAs or SSRIs appear to help the alcoholic addiction in alcohol-related disorder. It reduces the craving if given under medical supervision or after drug monitoring.

SSRIs: Modern antidepressants are useful in primary anxiety disorder in long term treatment. At the time of the crisis of anxiety, benzodiazepines are used as shock treatment. These are also used for panic disorder, generalized anxiety, post traumatic stress and eating behavior disorders.

MAOIs: These are used in the panic disorder, but because of their food interactions and less safety are less recommended.

SSRIs treatment in long term can be regulated the problem of insomnia and hence should be taken as lowest effective dose [16, 20].

Other Sources Having Antidepressant Effect

Hypericum: This plant is considered as a natural antidepressant, which is useful for mild depression. The withdrawal must be gradual. It exhibits interactions with other drugs [28].

Natural plants: Guarana, passion flower, ginger, valerian, willow, matte, hawthorn, sage meadows, mint, mentastro, chamomile, lemon balm and yarrow show medicinal properties.

Atypical antipsychotics: When there are psychotic symptoms such as mania, dementia or psychotic depression, then by using olanzapine, quetiapine, risperidone, clozapine and clotiapine, state of depression can be improved.

CONFLICT OF INTERESTS

The author confirms that this chapter contents have no conflict of interest.

ACKNOWLEDGEMENTS

I am grateful to Professor Dr. Antonio Zarzuelo Zurita. Thanks are also due to Department of Pharmacology, University of Pharmacy, Granada.

REFERENCES

[1] Dwight LE. Depression and bipolar disorders - Guide to the doctor, 1st ed., Mcgraw-Hill, 2007.
[2] Pasquini M, Berardelli I, Biondi M. Ethiopathogenesis of depressive disorders. Clin Pract Epidemiol Ment Health 2014; 10: 166-71.
[3] Olijslagers JE, Werkman TR, McCreary AC, Kruse CG, Wadman WJ. Modulation of midbrain dopamine neurotransmission by serotonin, a versatile interaction between neurotransmitters and significance for antipsychotic drug action. Curr Neuropharmacol 2006; 4: 59–68.
[4] Hashimoto K. Brain-derived neurotrophic factor (BDNF) and its precursor proBDNF as diagnostic biomarkers for major depressive disorder and bipolar disorder. Eur Arch Psychiatry Clin Neurosci 2015; 265: 83-84.
[5] Duckworth K, Hanson A. Using a clinical and evidence-based strategy to preserve access to psychiatric medications. Psychiatr Serv 2002; 53: 1231-2.
[6] Sánchez Peralta AM. Iron deficiency, Supplements and pharmaceutical care. Aula de la Farmacia. Grupo Saned 2012; 8.
[7] Lamberg L. Treating depression in medical conditions may improve quality of life. JAMA 1996; 276: 857-858.
[8] Sonnenberg E. Depression and chronic illness. What comes first? CVS Pharmacy. CVS Review. MSEd 2013.
[9] Miyoshi K. Depression associated with physical illness. JAMA 2001; 44: 279-282.
[10] Bryan Bruno MD, Dan V andIosifescu MD. Mood and Anxiety Disorders. Annals of Thoracic Surgery, news release 2013.
[11] Mitjans M, Arias B. The genetics of depression: What information can new methodologic approaches provide? Actas Esp Psiquiatr 2012; 40: 70-83.
[12] Continuing education for licensed pharmacists, Academy Abrente, Santiago de Compostela. Course: "Affective disorders in community pharmacy: depression and bipolar disorder." Pharmacotherapy. Accredited by the National Health System 2010.
[13] Michelle A. Clark, Richard A. Harvey, Richard Finkel, Jose A. Rey and Karen Whalen. Pharmacology, 5th ed, Lippincott Williams & Wilkins, Wolters Kluwer Health, 608 pages.
[14] Cohen LJ. Rational drug use in the treatment of depression. Pharmacotherapy 1997; 17: 45-61.
[15] Teixeira AL, de Souza RT, Zanetti M, *et al.* Increased plasma levels of soluble TNF receptors 1 and 2 in bipolar depression and impact of lithium treatment. Hum Psychopharmacol 2015; 30: 52-6.
[16] Fákáski M, Bjelik A, Hugyecz M, Kása P, Janka Z, Kálmán J. Imipramine and citalopram facilitate amyloid precursor protein secretion *in vitro*. Neurochem Int 2005; 47: 190-5.
[17] Culpepper L. Reducing the burden of difficult-to-treat major depressive disorder: Revisiting monoamine oxidase inhibitor therapy. Prim Care Companion CNS Disord 2013; 15.
[18] Austin MP, Mitchell PB. Use of psychotropic medications in breast-feeding women: acute and prophylactic treatment. Aust N Z J Psychiatry 1998; 32: 778-84.
[19] Vigod SN. Understanding and treating premenstrual dysphoric disorder: an update for the women's health practitioner. Obstet Gynecol Clin North Am 2009; 36: 907-924.
[20] Posner J, Hellerstein DJ, Gat I, *et al.* Antidepressants normalize the default mode network in patients with dysthymia. JAMA Psychiatry 2013; 70: 373-82.
[21] Kachko L, Ben Ami S, Liberman A, Birk E, Kronenberg S. Duloxetine contributing to a successful multimodal treatment program for peripheral femoral neuropathy and comorbid 'reactive depression' in an adolescent. Pain Res Manag 2011; 16: 457-9.
[22] Stein MB, Kirk P, Prabhu V, Grott M, Terepa M. Mixed anxiety-depression in a primary-care clinic. J Affect Disord 1995; 34: 79-84.
[23] Rice A. Common Therapeutic Factors in Bereavement Groups. Death Stud 2014.

[24] Reinhardt MM, Cohen CI. Late-life psychosis: diagnosis and treatment. Curr Psychiatry Rep 2015; 17: 542

[25] Noone D, Ames C, Hassanali N, *et al.* A preliminary investigation of schematic beliefs and unusual experiences in children. Eur Psychiatry 2015.

[26] Petit J, Sansone RA. A case of interdose discontinuation symptoms with venlafaxine extended release. The Primary Care Companion to CNS Disorders 2011; 13: 5.

[27] Pacheco L, Aragües M, Malo P, *et al.* Alternatives in the management of discontinuation syndrome with new antidepressants. Psiquiatria Biologica 2002; 9: 133-41.

[28] Catalogue of Medicinal Products. General Council of Associations of Pharmacists, Madrid, Spain 2013.

CHAPTER 2

P300 Wave in Depression: An Update

Ravi Prakash[1,*], Srinivasa R.[2] and Priyanka Rastogi[3]

[1]Department of Physiology, M.S. Ramaiah Medical College, Bangalore, India; [2]Department of Neurology M.S. Ramaiah Medical College, Bangalore, India and [3]Sai Krupa Hospital Mathikere Bangalore, India

Abstract: Event related potentials (ERP) are generated in response to a distinct episode such as when a sensory stimulus is present or there is cognitive reaction for such a stimulus. The electrical potentials generated from such motor, sensory or cognitive events are called electroencephalographic (EEG) fluctuation. Electrically, these are the reflection of the combined activity of postsynaptic potentials generated by huge number (measuring thousands or millions in number) of cortical pyramidal neurons which are oriented in a similar manner and are firing in synchrony. Among all the event related potentials, the best studied has been that of the positive wave arising at around 300 ms, popularly known as the P300. The P300 is the positive wave appearing at about 300 ms after presentation of stimulus. This ERP component was first explained by Sutton *et al.* and is extensively examined in relation to neurophysiological evaluation of cognitive functions. They described this waveform in terms of amplitude, polarity and latency. Many studies have reported that depressed individuals have distinctive cognitive impairment. The impact of these findings was such that the cognitive impairment of decreased ability to concentrate has become one of the nine core DSM-IV diagnostic criteria for major depressive disorder as a characteristic feature of syndromal depression. Perhaps next to schizophrenia, depression has been the most studied psychiatric condition to be evaluated with P300. So far, more than 20 studies have analysed the P300 component in depressed individuals and have unanimously pointed that depression causes an attenuated P300 response for different stimulus types and sensory modalities-auditory tones, geometric shapes, alphanumeric characters, nonsense syllables and photographs. The use of P300 in depression has been mainly for two purposes- 1) Diagnostic and 2) Prognostic. In this review, we will elaborate these findings of P300 in depression and their applications.

Keywords: Depression, event related potential, P300 wave.

EVENT RELATED POTENTIAL P300-AN INTRODUCTION

Event-related potentials (ERPs) are small electrical potentials measuring in micro volts recorded from the scalp. These potentials are generated in the superficial cortical areas whenever there is some particular stimulus or other event [1]. On

***Corresponding author Ravi Prakash:** Department of Physiology M.S. Ramaiah Medical College, Bangalore, India; Tel: +919620552673; E-mail: rprakashneuro@hotmail.com

Puneetpal Singh and Sarabjit Mastana (Eds)

recording, these are visible in the form of troughs and peaks intermingled with background Electroencephalogram (EEG) waves. The potentials are generated in response to a distinct event like 1) presence of a sensory stimulus or 2) cognitive reaction to a sensory stimulus. The electroencephalographic (EEG) waves that are actually electrical potentials produced in response to motor, sensory or cognitive events. The recording of EEG waves proves to be a safe and non-invasive approach for studying psycho - physiological attributes of mental activities. These are the reflection of combined activity of postsynaptic potentials generated by a huge number (measuring thousands or millions in number) of cortical pyramidal neurons that are oriented in a similar way and are firing in synchrony [2]. There are several ways to classify ERPs. The most prevalent method of categorizing ERP waves divides it into two types: sensory and cognitive. Sensory or exogenous waves are those which are produced within 100 milliseconds after giving stimulus. These are mostly affected by the physical parameters of the stimulus. On the other hand, ERPs generated beyond 100 ms of stimulus presentation reflect the more sophisticated process of cognitive evaluation of the stimulus. As these represent the sensory information processing by the brain, hence are known as 'cognitive' or 'endogenous' ERPs. The nomenclature of these wave forms have been traditionally done according to latency and order of appearance. Among all the event related potentials, the best studied has been that of the positive wave arising at around 300 ms, popularly known as the P300. It was first described by Sutton *et al.* [3], who described this waveform in terms of amplitude, polarity and latency as he described it as "*the major waveform alteration in the amplitude of the positive- going component which reaches peak amplitude at about 300 ms*". Consequently, within a short period of the crucial features of the P300 were determined. The fact that peak latency of P300 occurs at 300 ms after a stimulus is presented to a subject where he has to make an effort of sensory discrimination, gave it the designated name. Also, it is the third major positive peak in the later part of any evoked potential gave it another designation as P3 wave. Sutton *et al.* [4] observed that P300 wave could be evoked by excluding a stimulus if this exclusion was informative. Subsequently, Ritter and Vaughan [5] used for the first time, the "oddball" paradigm, wherein a subject has to detect rare target signals that are intermixed randomly among the more frequent standard stimuli being presented at fixed intervals. At the same time, the authors were also studying the scalp distribution of this wave and found that it was mainly distributed over the parieto-central area [6]. The further details of this waveform and its neuropsychological as well as neurophysiological correlates are described in next sections. Briefly, P300 wave is a parieto-central positivity of ERP which is produced on consciously detecting an informative task-relevant stimulus by a subject. This wave has contributed a plethora of information on the fundamental neural activities underlying the cognitive processes [3, 7]. Despite hundreds of studies conducted since its discovery, the P300 is not used practically for assessment purposes and remains controversial because its neural generators are still imprecise.

THE RECORDING OF P300-MEASURES AND CONVENTIONS

Event-related potentials (ERPs) are typically recorded from the scalp with standard EEG electrodes and amplifiers. ERPs can be generated by a large number of sensory, cognitive, or motor events. Because ERP is superimposed on the ongoing EEG, it is often difficult to see an ERP in a single sample. Therefore in the typical strategy, the repeated presentation of an eliciting event and the subject's average ERP is yielded by averaging the emerging ERPs (coordinated at the point of time of evoking event), so that the activity not time- locked to the eliciting event averages out (*i.e.*, to zero), and what remains is the series of waves time locked to the stimulus.

Depending upon the number of stimuli presented, several different paradigms have been designed for elicitation of ERP waves (Fig. **1**). In *the single- stimulus task*, the target is exposed occasionally in time with no other stimuli. In the traditional *two-stimulus oddball task*, the frequently presented standard stimuli is accompanied by another occasional stimulus. In the *three-stimulus oddball,* the target is presented alongwith two more stimuli; one is standard stimuli which occurs frequently and the other is distracter stimuli which occurs infrequently. In this the subject has to respond physically or mentally only to the target stimulus while not responding to any other stimuli. Further modifications have been included in these paradigms for altering the task difficulty. A large positive potential is seen by the target in each case, whose amplitude increases from the frontal to parietal electrodes, which peaks at about 300 ms for auditory and 400 ms for visual target stimuli in young adults [8, 9].

The recording of ERP is conducted using the scalp electrodes by positioning them on the surface of the skull, according to the International 10-20 System (SI 10-20) of the American Society of Electroencephalography [10]. At present, no consensus has been reached regarding the positioning and number of the live electrodes required for recording ERP. While many researchers use one electrode by placing on Cz [11-13], others advocate the use of two live electrodes, placed on Fz and Cz [14, 15], Fz and Pz [16], or some place on Fz, Cz and Pz by

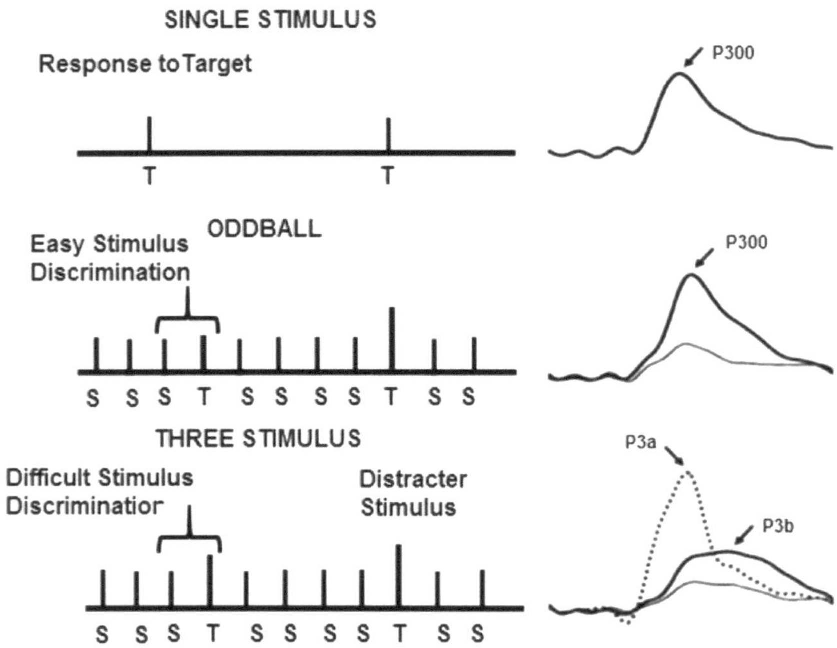

Fig. (1). Schematic illustration of the single-stimulus (top), oddball (middle), and three-stimulus (bottom) paradigms, along with the consequent 4 ERPs elicited from the stimuli of each task at the right. S- Standard stimulus T- Target stimulus.

using three live electrodes [17]. Positioning of the electrodes carries immense importance because of great variability observed in the latency of P300 component among various positions. The observed waveform on ERP is described in terms of the measures of amplitude, latency and scalp distribution. These measures are described as follows:

"*Amplitude* (µV) is defined as the difference between the mean pre- stimulus baseline voltage and the largest positive- going peak of the ERP waveform within a time window (*e.g.*, 250-500 ms, although the range can vary depending on stimulus modality, task conditions, subject age, *etc.*)."

"*Latency* (ms) is defined as the time from stimulus onset to the point of maximum positive amplitude within a time window.

Scalp distribution for P300 is defined as the amplitude change over the midline electrodes (Fz, Cz, Pz), which typically increases in magnitude from the frontal to parietal electrode sites" [18].

THE NORMAL P300 WAVEFORM AND ITS COGNITIVE BASIS

As mentioned before, normal P300 waveform appears as a positive deflection at around 300 ms after presentation of the stimulus. Historically, P300 has been considered as a conglomerate of two components; an early component known as P3a and a later component which has been named as the P3b. P3a can be acquired by an occasional tone alongwith another frequent tone observed in the absence of a discrimination task which is physically different, usually observed as a positive waveform having relatively short peak latency and a central/parietal maximum amplitude distribution. This component has been named the "P3a" to distinguish it from the task-relevant target "P3b"potential [19, 20]. The most prominent and well-characterized component of P300 is P3b, popularly known as the "classical P3" which in contrary to P3a is typified by frontally-oriented topography and shorter latencies [19, 21]. P3a does not seem to be related to the discrimination task. Therefore, the P3a has been observed directly during oddball task processing in only 10-20 % of normal young adults [22]. Additionally, a P3a-like potential is also produced by auditory and visual stimuli presented without a task [8, 23]. However, one group of researchers has deviated from this two-component view of P300. For example, Simons *et al.* [24] found no differences between the two components after careful replication of the original non- novel stimulus of auditory P3a [19] and novelty P300 tasks [25].

Inspite of these reports, a much larger group of studies still maintains the view that P300 consists of two components which become prominent as the difficulty of the task increases. The controversy prevails in this context as the neurological investigations remain equivocal in their findings. According to ERP waveform factor analysis Novelty P3 and P3a are same [24], whereas, the cortical potential imaging methods for modeling the responses to auditory stimuli are in support of the hypothesis that the two components are temporally and spatially distinct [26].

Over the years, enough data has accumulated to strengthen the view that some cortical cognitive processing underlies the generation of P300. The details of these cognitive activities are discussed in next sections. Both the peak latency as well as the component latencies reflects with cognitive efficiency. For example, when checked in normal subjects, it has negative correlation with superior performance on neuropsychological tests of immediate memory [27-29].

However, this association of P300 measures with immediate memory seems to be an oversimplification.

P300 measures are affected by many other cognitive factors also, for example, task relevance/difficulty, stimulus information content and sequence probability structure [30, 31]. Putting all these cognitive domains in one single model for explaining the P300 is too complicated right now. However, some theories have attempted it. We will address few of these theories here.

THE CONTEXT UPDATE HYPOTHESIS

The most prevalent interpretation of P300 wave is that it acts as an index to the brain actions and appears on the updation of mental representation of the stimulus environment [32]. This concept is developed from Sokolov's model of the '*orienting response*' which is further derived from habituation and dishabituation effects [33]. This same mechanism has been implicated in explaining the origin of P300 waveform [9, 34]. This theory propounds that initial sensory processing is followed by the comparison of the current stimulus to the previously presented stimulus in the 'working memory'. If there is no change regarding stimulus, the old stimulus "*schema*" is maintained, and sensory evoked potentials are recorded as usual. On the other hand, more sophisticated attention mechanisms are employed on the processing of a new stimulus, that result in the "*updating*" of the memory representation for the stimulus context thereby eliciting the event related potential generation of P300 [35]. As larger P300 amplitudes arise for earlier stimuli in the memory, so these events are also considered to be associated with long-term storage, [36, 37]. Thus the parameters of P300 have been implicated in measuring the attributes of this updating process. Therefore, the P300 latency is believed to be a measure of stimulus classification speed. However, this parameter is unrelated to response selection processes [38].

The adaptability of the context-updating hypothesis has been its major theoretical strength. This is evident by the fact that even after 25 years of this concept and further confirmations, it has not been refuted although other theoretical perspectives have emerged [39-41]. The context-updating approach depicts that P3a is significantly associated with strong initial target stimulus processing and it diminishes when P3b is produced by the repeated target stimuli [42].

THE RESOURCE ALLOCATION HYPOTHESIS

The derivation of context-updating hypothesis of P300 has largely been done by managing the probability of target stimulus in two-stimulus oddball tasks.

Segregating the target from the ongoing standard sequence of stimulus results in the production of a robust P300 whose amplitude increases with decrease in probability of targets global and local sequence [43-45]. An additional observation noted in subsequent studies was that the amount of attentional resources employed during dual-task performance affect P300 amplitude. A dual task paradigm typically consists of a primary and a secondary task. The primary task is performance of varied cognitive demands and at the same time subject is also mentally involved in a secondary task of counting target oddball stimuli. It has been observed in several studies that irrespective of modality or the motor requirements of the primary task, P300 amplitude decreases with the increase in the primary task difficulties [46-48]. In neuropsychological terms, the overall arousal level, administering the amount of attention available for task performance changes the information processing system [49]. When task conditions are undemanding, P300 amplitude theoretically reflects the enhanced use of attentional resources for the tasks thereby resulting in relatively large amplitude and short peak latency. On the other hand, the tasks requiring greater attentional resources, use up the processing resources, hence, peak latency is longer and P300 amplitude is smaller [42, 50]. Further, modulation of P300 depends on the availability of attention processes which are affected by trait and state arousal levels [51]. These trait and state arousal effects have also been termed as tonic and phasic arousal levels where former occur in minutes or hours and are expressions of comparatively slow fluctuations in the energetic arousal state and latter on the other hand reveal an individual's energetic reaction to particular stimulus events thereby affecting the availability of attentional resources and thus the P300 measures [42, 52]. Hence, tonic and phasic arousal effects originate from spontaneous and situational factors respectively thereby affecting the P300 measures. These factors are important as they can be manipulated to increase experimental sensitivity and to reduce individual variations [52].

RELATION OF P300 WITH MEMORY

The origins of the attention allocation and orienting response effects for P300 led to assessment of the relations between P300 and recall memory to performance [53]. Typically in this paradigm, words are shown in a serial pattern and ERPs are recorded. Sometimes, stimulus distinctiveness is induced by changing font size of one or two words than the other words, which affects the encoding and facilitates the recall memory. It was found that this distinct stimulus provided recall and evoked larger P300 components during encoding as compared to those that were not recalled. However, when participants used rote rehearsal, the component amplitude was larger for subsequent recall, which shows that P300 was affected by the rehearsal strategy [54]. On the other hand, when on employing an elaborative strategy, it was observed that subsequent recall performance has no effect on P300 amplitude. On the basis of these findings the authors concluded that P300 amplitude is affected by tasks altering stimulus attention and requiring fundamental memory processing [55]. Additionally, it has been observed that studied word stimuli receiving full attention are perceived with more confidence and are associated with greater P300 amplitude [56]. Furthermore, the items evoking a late positive potential exhibit larger memory than those eliciting lesser potential [34, 57] further strengthening the associations between P300 and memory recall. Finally, the delay in the retrieval in a serial position paradigm shows persistent close relationship of P300 amplitude with encoding mechanisms which endorses the view that this potential is associated with engagement of memory networks. Thus, the relationship between P300 and memory can be concluded by stating that increased P300 amplitude is produced by stimulus encoding which promotes successful memory storage to facilitate recognition and retrieval. Näätänen [58] proposed that the P3b component indexes memory storage as well as serves as a link between attention and stimulus characteristics.

Thus at present, a perfectly integrated picture of the cognitive factors associated with P300 related neural processing has not yet been modeled. However, it can be stated that P300 is associated with overall cognitive processing. This is especially strengthened by the fact that the conditions where cognitive processing are impaired also result in impairments in P300 latency and amplitude. Thus, P300 latency increases with normal aging [59, 60], whereas with decline in mental capability because of dementia peak timing increases [61-63]. It can also be altered with alert mechanisms, state of conscience, deficits in the selective attention and psychological conditions that impair attention [64, 65]. As discussed above, when the attention focus required for the primary discrimination task is interrupted by an infrequent non target stimulus event which may not be novel, the P3a is produced.

THE NEUROPHYSIOLOGY OF P300

The Neural Origin of P300

Like the neuropsychology of P300, its neurophysiology remains unclear at many levels. This is because the neural generators of P300 are not thoroughly defined, though much work has been done in the last 25 years [66-68]. The electroencephalogram (EEG) supposedly reflects the summed up response of postsynaptic potentials generated by enormous cortical pyramidal neurons (in thousands or millions) oriented in a same manner, firing in synchrony while processing information [2]. It is considered that multiple generators play role towards P300 Long Latency Auditory Evoked Potential, such as in the case of component N2, the supratemporal cortex, and the reticular formation, thalamus, frontal cortex, primary cortex, hippocampus, lemniscus, inferior colliculus and centro-parietal cortex [64, 65]. Also, it is not associated to the activity of the individual's memory but to information processing [69]. As it was believed that the predominant memory and attention related operations were associated with P300 generation, it is not surprising that the earliest human studies focused on the hippocampal formation for exploring the neural origins of ERP. In these studies, for determining the sources of epileptic foci in patients, depth electrodes were implanted. The recordings confirmed the generation of at least some portion of the P300 (P3b) in the hippocampal areas of the medial temporal lobe [70, 71]. Nonetheless, further studies used scalp recordings on individuals after temporal lobectomy [37, 72] and experimental excisions in monkeys alongwith studies on patients subserving severe medial temporal lobe damage observed that the P300 generation is not directly associated to hippocampal formation [73-75]. Surely, non significant differences for P300 amplitude or latency were observed, when patients with bilateral hippocampal lesions compared to a matched control group [76]. However, current view regarding the involvement of hippocampus in P300 has become more evolved by the recent study results. Presently it is opined that the hippocampal formation plays role in "novelty" information processing. This opinion is mainly derived from the patients with focal hippocampal lesions who exhibited low P3a amplitude from novel distracters whereas normal P3b components were generated from targets [77]. More sophisticated source-analysis techniques have also pointed towards the Hippocampus as the site of origin for P3a. Quadruple-dipole modelling of somatosensory-evoked that P3b has restricted its origin explicitly to the parietal cortical and hippocampal regions [78]. Another analysis of auditory- evoked potentials *via* brain electric source analysis and multiple- dipole 10 modelling indicated putative generators in the temporal lobe and hippocampus [79].

However, in spite of the contributory role of hippocampus, currently the universally accepted site of origin of P300 is the frontal lobe of brain. There are several lines of evidences showing that it is mainly the frontal lobe which is associated with the generation of P300. Neuropsychological evidences point towards this direction hypothesizing that in an oddball paradigm the process of discriminating between target and standard stimuli requires the frontal lobe activity that is mainly sensitive to the attentional demands stimulated by task performance [80, 81]. This is assumed to start activity in the frontal lobe which employs the attention focus as desired by task performance [80, 81]. fMRI and ERP findings have confirmed that frontal lobe activity is involved for the detection of physically alerting or rare stimuli [82, 83]. Neuropathological studies also support these findings.

Patients suffering from lesions in the frontal lobe exhibited a parietal maximum for P3b and an attenuation of P3a amplitude., This further endorses that for P3a generation frontal lobe integrity is necessary [84, 85]. Further studies on humans with frontal lobe lesions have provided evidence that in such patients target stimulus generates a clear parietal maximum for the P3b, whereas, the distracter stimulus causes decrease of P3a [84]. When lesion patients were compared to controls for P3a amplitude from novel auditory distracter stimuli, it was observed to be virtually eliminated over frontal electrode sites, whereas, for P3b amplitude from the target stimulus no differences were observed between the two groups.

In addition to the frontal lobe, temporo-parietal junction is another area which has been implicated in association to P300. Although no direct link has been established between the two, it has been observed that integrity of temporo - parietal junction affects the P300 amplitude and the absence of this integrity greatly reduces the component size over the parietal area [85, 86]. This association has been implied in proposing that there can be a circuit pathway between temporal/parietal and frontal brain which could be contributing for the generation of P3a and P3b [68, 87, 88]. This area has also been implicated neuropsychologically. For example, P3b appears when memory operations are promoted in temporo-parietal areas by successive attentional resource activations [74, 89]. Indeed, cellular recording studies in primates point out that information generated by frontal activation changes during a matching- to-sample task is forced to infero-temporal structures that index task context updating for future stimulus presentations [90]. This supports the concept that frontal and temporal/parietal activation originates from P3a and P3b generation activation [91].

This view supports the previous neurocognitive theory that top-down attention switching is invoked by the incoming stimuli and response organization and production are guided by the bottom-up memory-driven operations [92, 93]. Further studies on ERP and fMRI proposed that neural responsivity to novelty is managed by frontal attention mechanism [94-96] involving top-down control by that [97-99].

Response organization which is produced by bottom-up processing lead to the production of attentional resources that control memory items in parietal regions [39, 40]. These findings were further endorsed by the fact that there is a loss of the P3b waveform with physical lesion to tissue in the temporal- parietal junction [87, 100]. Recordings by invasive cerebral electrode have shown that classical P300 is generated in the temporal-parietal junction. Lesion studies have also shown that following the hippocampal activity, the integrity of the temporal-parietal lobe junction is required in either the generation or transmission processes thereby contributing to the generation of ERP [100, 101].

Thus, an integrated picture of the origin and propagation of P300 will involve the two of the brain areas: frontal lobe and the parieto-temporal area. In fact, the neuro-electrical actions underlying P300 generation originate from some yet unclear interaction between frontal lobe and hippocampal /temporal- parietal function [74, 91]. Some studies have revealed that the patterns of parietal and frontal -to-temporal lobe activation are similar to those produced by ERP and fMRI studies using oddball tasks [26, 102]. Magnetic resonance imaging (MRI) of gray matter volumes corroborates the association of the size of frontal lobe area with individual variation in P3a amplitude from distracter stimuli, whereas parietal area size corresponds to P3b amplitude from target stimuli [103]. Such results may underlie individual P3a and P3b variability [19, 104].

Other brain areas have also been implicated in P300. P3a appears to be related to the neural changes in the anterior cingulate gyrus when incoming stimuli replace the contents of working memory and effect of this representational change is transmitted to infero-temporal lobe representation maintenance mechanisms [90]. Principal component analysis isolates the Supplementary Motor Cortex (SMC) or cingulate gyrus as generators for the Novelty P3 [105]. The memory storage operations which are initiated in the formation of hippocampus generate P3b and its updated result is transmitted to parietal cortex [74, 89]. Thus, P3a is produced when frontal lobe attention gets instruction from a demanding stimulus whereas P3b is produced when attention resources are allocated for memory updating in association cortex. An important aspect of P300 generation is the communication of information between the two cerebral hemispheres. Thus the role of corpus callosum becomes evidently important. In fact, it has been proposed that as P300 amplitude is larger over the right compared to left frontal/central areas, so right frontal cortex is the place from where activation of the neural stimulation during auditory oddball discrimination may initiate [8, 106]. Once the incoming stimulus is processed in the frontal area, there is propagation of activity between the cerebral hemispheres across the corpus callosum [107]. Further evidence is provided by different studies showing that left handed individuals having larger callosal fibre tracts exhibit larger P300 amplitudes and shorter latencies than right-handed individuals [108, 109] as these two groups differ in their corpus callosum size [110].

It is thought that at cellular level P300 is composed of a series of neuronal sub networks developing at differing rates. Traumatic or other insult to the prefrontal cortex causes decreased amplitude of the novelty P3 response to a novel stimulus [84], which is further correlated with reduced attentional shift towards novel stimuli [94]. Schematic representation of brain areas hypothesized as being neural generators for P300. The areas numbered as follows: 1) Midline frontal cortex 2) Anterior temporal cortex 3) Superior and 4) Inferior parietal cortices 5) Anterior cingulate cortex and 6) Hippocampus

THE GENETIC UNDERPINNINGS OF P300

It has been found that the specific personality attributes such as impulsivity, sensation seeking and introversion/extraversion alongwith the conclusions for ERPs are in accordance to genetic underpinnings for P300 [111, 112].

Individual variations regarding personality-related arousal levels have been observed to show correlation with P300, where low arousal individuals (requiring high intensity stimulus for being aroused) have smaller P300 amplitudes as compared to high-arousal individuals having larger P300 components [113, 114]. Of course this relationship is not linear and is modulated by several factors including the biological factors [52], differences among paradigms used [115], and psychopathology [116-118]. How these genetic influences could be transferred to the neurophysiological variables like P300 remains a matter of debate. However, some speculations have been made. For example,individual variability for neurotransmitter function gives rise to differences for attentional resource capabilities, which can cause such effects [119, 120].

AN OVERVIEW OF PHYSIOLOGICAL VARIATIONS OF P300

The physiological variations of P300 could be either intra individual or inter-individual. It is important to mention here that there could be differences in the

P300 parameters in a single individual over the course of time. This process known as *'habituation'* refers to the fact that familiarization with repeated stimuli affects P300 parameters [34]. Stimulus-dependent variation of the P300 measures is another reason for the intra-individual variation in P300. A plethora of evidence supports the fact that the nature of the stimulus affects P300 properties [121]. This stimulus related alteration could be because of exogenous factors including the probability of presentation [43], sequence of stimuli [122], stimulus quality, target-to-target time interval (TTI) [123] as well as due to the endogenous factors resulting from the stimulus related variables like attention, task relevance of the stimulus [124] and the time involved in evaluation of the stimulus [123].

There is a delayed reaction time in response to non-matching word/colour combinations when exposed to word *vs*. colour "Stroop" tasks in which a verbal response is required, but no change in latency was observed [125, 126]. Finally, regarding changes in the internal physiologic state of subjects, like physical activity, natural circadian and ultradian rhythms to levels of fatigue, intra-individual variations in P300 have been found [52]. Interestingly, a study investigated the effect of winter, spring, and summer seasons on P300 amplitude and found that there is an indirect relationship of seasonal ambient sunlight with P300 amplitude and women are observed to experience larger shifts than men [127]. These variations could be the reason of the test-retest correlation coefficient of P300 in normal individuals being less than 1. This variability could be from ultradian rhythm effects on ERP measures [34]. In spite of this variation, P300 is also sensitive to most standard biomedical clinical assays, which can assess difference between normal and patient populations regarding individual cognitive capability and are relatively inexpensive to record [128].

Coming to the inter-individual variations, the two major physiological variables affecting the P300 measures have been the age and gender of the individual. These two variables must be taken into account when analyzing the P300-Long Latency Auditory Evoked Potential.

For younger age groups, it has been observed that, in normal individuals with age ranging between eight and eleven years, the P3 component latency is increased in proportionality to age which was however, not statistically significant [129]. For adult individuals, it is almost an accepted fact that the P300 latency increases with age where as the amplitude decreases (this decrease is very modest). However, authors are divided in their views regarding that if these changes are linear with age progression. Another important age-related variation of P300 is the shift of its location on scalp as is seen in aged subjects where P300 amplitude is shifted more towards the frontal region [130].

Regarding the gender related variations, some studies [22, 131] did not find statistically significant differences. However, another set of studies have showed gender specific differences, with females having lower mean P3 component latency values and standard deviation than males [132]. Some evidences exist to show that when left-handed subjects were compared to right-handers, greater amplitude and smaller latencies are observed for auditory and visual stimulus discrimination tasks. Aerobic exercise also increases P300 amplitude sharply [133]; but is not affected by food intake in relation to other ERPs [134].

COGNITIVE DEFICITS IN DEPRESSION

Large number of studies have shown that depressed individuals exhibit distinctive cognitive impairment [135-137]. The impact of these findings was such that the cognitive impairment of decreased ability to concentrate has been included in the nine core DSM-IV diagnostic symptoms for major depressive disorder (American Psychiatric Association, 1994) as a characteristic feature of syndromal depression. In depression, attention is the most extensively studied domain of cognitive function. Most of these studies have spanned from late 1980s to 2000s and have reported unanimously that depressed patients experience significant impairments of attentional function [138-140]. The exact reason for these impairments remains unknown. One view suggests that due to the state of depression there is a decrease in available attentional resources which leads to these impairments. The impairments in the ability to filter out distracting stimuli could be a contributing factor [141-143]. Such functions have great clinical implications, as these deteriorate the ability of a person suffering from depression to work normally in employment and social settings. Also, these cause hindrances in psychotherapy as well as restrict them from adhering to pharmacology regimen. However, there is a lack of published reports on the above mentioned types of cognitive dysfunction occurring in depression and the way these are linked functionally.

There have been much fewer attempts to clarify the reasons and nature of these attentional impairments in depression. An interesting correlation between the cognitive bias and cognitive impairments has been recently made [144]. They proposed that the decreased attentional function in depressed individuals could possibly be because of two reasons: (a) "as a general, pervasive impairment in attentional function or (b) as evidence of a relative attentional deficit, *i.e.*, regarding only stimuli that are not negatively valent (stimuli that are not of particular salience to depressed individuals given their preferential bias for the processing of negatively toned information)."However, till date, most of these theories remain mere speculations and more organized data are yet to emerge.

P300 IN DEPRESSION

The event related potential P300 has been studied in almost all of the psychiatric conditions for evaluation of cognitive functions of such patients. Perhaps next to schizophrenia, depression has been the most studied psychiatric condition to be evaluated with P300. The classical finding in 16 patients suffering from major depression has been the reduction in P300 amplitudes [145, 146]. Interestingly, when patients with major depression were treated with antidepressants, they exhibited normalized P300 amplitudes [147]. This finding is in contrast to that seen in the patients with schizophrenia, when treated with antipsychotic medication, showed reduced P300 amplitudes that reflected both the state and the trait of the disease [148].

More than 20 reports have been published so far which have investigated the P300 component in relation to depression and have unanimously pointed towards an attenuated P300 response in depression when exposed to different stimuli and sensory modalities—auditory tones [149-151], geometric shapes, alphanumeric characters [152, 153], nonsense syllables [154] and photographs [155]. Some of these studies and their relevant findings have been included in Table **1**. However, there are some studies which have produced conflicting findings in this context. For example, [156] no significant differences were found in the P300 parameters between those suffering from depression and the healthy controls. Recently P300 has been looked at from the angle of the negativistic attentional bias in depression or by the more fancy name of "*depressotypic*" attentional impairment. This angle has largely been overlooked in the field of research. However, one study has used stimuli of negative emotional valence for evaluating the P300 response, where it was observed that reduction in P300 was not in response to stimulus words of negative valence [157]. This result would have been of immense significance in explicating the nature of depressotypic attentional impairment, but it had two major limitations [158] which acts as a flaw in its interpretability: (a) the individuals were categorised as ''depressed'' using self- reported instrument only instead of employing a structured diagnostic Interview [159] and (b) stimulus presentation in a task format not ideally suited to evoke P300 component (*i.e.*, non- oddball task).

Table 1. P300 related studies in depression.

Sample Size	Paradigm	Study Design	Relevant Findings	Study
Depressed = 25 Controls = 25	Auditory and visual oddball P300 tasks	Cross-sectional	Significantly decreased amplitudes of P300 in depressed	Pfefferbaum *et al.* (1984) [146]
Dementia = 19 Depressed = 17 Schizophrenia = 15	Auditory oddball P300 task	Cross-sectional	Prolonged P300 latencies in the depressed subjects	Gordon *et al.* (1986) [160]
Depressed =16 Controls =59	Auditory discrimination Task	Cross-sectional	the P3 latency did not differ from that of controls. P3 amplitude was reduced in the acutely depressed	Blackwood *et al.* (1987) [145]
Depressed = 8 Normal older = 15 Normal young=12	Auditory odd-ball P300 task	Cross-sectional	Variable P300 latencies	Patterson *et al.* (1988) [161]
Depressed = 26 Controls = 26	Measurement of the Bereitschaft's potential	Cross-sectional	The amplitude and frequency are lower in subjects with melancholic depression compared to the healthy controls	Khanna *et al.* (1989) [162]
Depressed = 20 Controls = 20	Auditory odd-ball paradigm	Cross-sectional	The latency of P300 was found to be significantly delayed in cases of major depression as compared to that of controls.	Himani *et al.* (1999) [163]
Depressed = 22 Controls = 22	Two-tone-discrimination task	Cross-sectional	None of the group differences in latency were statistically significant	Kraiuhin *et al.* (1990) [164]
Depressed = 27 Controls = 27	Auditory discrimination task	Cross-sectional and case-control study	No significant differences in any of the ERP measures	Sara *et al.* (1994) [156]
Depressed (DSM III) = 40 Controls = 40		Cross-sectional and case-control study	Depressives had a significantly prolonged P300 latency and reduced P300 amplitude as compared to the controls.	Singh *et al.* (2000) [165]
Depressed (Melancholic) = 50 Controls = 31	Auditory odd-ball P300 task	Cross-sectional and case-control study	The melancholic group showed a significantly higher latency in P300 and a significantly lower P300 amplitude than healthy controls	Urretavizcaya *et al.* (2003) [166]
Depressed = 36 Controls = 20	Auditory odd-ball P300 task	Cross-sectional and case-control study	P300 latencies were significantly prolonged both in patients with and without psychotic features compared to controls	Karaaslan *et al.* (2003) [167]
Depressed = 53 Controls = 40	Auditory oddball P300 task	Cross-sectional and case-control study	A smaller P3b in non-responders *versus* both responders and controls	Jaworska *et al.* (2013) [168]

APPLICATIONS OF P300 IN DEPRESSION

The use of P300 in depression has been mainly for two purposes- 1) Diagnostic and 2) Prognostic.

Regarding the diagnostic use, P300 evaluation of depressed patients was prominent in 1970s. However, the current trend has been focused on individual symptom evaluation using P300 rather than the whole condition of depression. For example, Urretavizcaya *et al.* [166] investigated the differences between the event related potentials of normal individuals and melancholic patients. They observed that a significantly higher latency as well as ERP waveforms like N100, N200, P300 and significantly lower P300 amplitude was produced in melancholic group as compared to the healthy controls. However, the latencies of the N400 or their inter latencies showed no differences. No significant correlations were found between HDRS and DRRS scores with amplitude or latency measures. Additionally, there were no associations between these abnormalities and the clinical variables.

The authors found it difficult to make any conclusion out of it due to the limitations in their study. They mentioned that all the subjects of this study were inpatients and not random, with a severe subcategory of depression and the value of average age was also high. Therefore, these findings could not be generalized. Similarly, Karaaslan *et al.* [167] investigated the possible differences in the P300 component of event-related potentials in depressed patients in relation to psychotic features and to check the effect of treatment if any on these changes. They found that the pretreatment P300 latencies were significantly prolonged in both type of patients *i.e.* with and without psychotic features as compared to controls. However, the patients with psychotic features exhibited significantly decreased pretreatment P300 amplitudes and not in those without psychotic features.

In past few years, there has been more effort directed towards the use of this data for evaluating the depression patients prognostically rather than for diagnostic purposes. In the study by Vandoolaeghe *et al.* [169], significantly higher P300 latency and P200 amplitude was observed in the patients suffering from major depression with normal cognition when compared to normal volunteers. However, significantly lower P300 latency was found when these patients were compared with major depressed patients having cognitive impairment, although, AERP components showed no significant changes upon subchronic treatment with antidepressants. Those who did not respond to the antidepressant therapy had significantly higher pretreatment P300 latency and P200 amplitude as compared to the treatment responders and normal volunteers. The authors concluded that major depression is accompanied by delayed P300 latency as well as increased P200 amplitude and may predict a nonresponsive to subsequent anti-depressive therapy.

Recently, Jaworska *et al.* [168] observed that non-responders to antidepressant treatment had smaller baseline P3a/b amplitudes than responders and healthy controls. By week 12 baseline P3b amplitude also gave weekly predictions of the extent of depression rating changes. More target hits were reported in controls as compared to non-responders with reference to task performance. ERP measures showed correlation with clinical changes in males and with behavioral measures in females. These results corroborate the fact that a positive antidepressant response is associated with greater (or control-like) baseline P3a/b amplitudes. On the other hand, studies have shown that the delayed P300 can be best understood as the state marker of depression. For example, Murty *et al.* [170] found that P300 amplitudes were smaller in depressed patients and this abnormality normalized after recovery. Similarly, Karaaslan *et al.* [167] observed that after being treated for depression, delayed P300 latencies in patients and decreased P300 amplitude in the patient group with psychotic features became normalized.

Based on these findings, they concluded that prolonged P300 latency can be considered a state marker for major depressive episode and decreased P300 amplitude having correlation with paranoid ideation might have a more evident presence in the psychotic subtype of depression.

CONFLICT OF INTERESTS

The authors confirm that this chapter contents have no conflict of interest.

ACKNOWLEDGEMENTS

Declared None.

REFERENCES

[1] Blackwood DHR, Muir WJ. Cognitive brain potentials and their application. Brit J Psychiatry 1990; 157: 96-101.
[2] Peterson NN, Schroeder CE, Arezzo JC. Neural generators of early cortical somatosensory evoked potentials in the awake monkey. Electroencephalog Clin Neurophysiol 1995; 96: 248-260.
[3] Sutton S, Braren M, Zubin J, John E. Evoked potential correlates of stimulus uncertainty. Science 1965; 150: 1187-1188.

[4] Sutton S, Tueting P, Zubin J. Information delivery and the sensory evoked potential. Science 1967; 155: 1436-1439.

[5] Ritter W, Vaughan HG. Averaged evoked responses in vigilance and discrimination: a reassessment. Science 1969; 164: 326-328.

[6] Vaughan HG, Ritter W. The sources of auditory evoked responses recorded from the human scalp. Electroencephalogr Clin Neuro 1970; 28: 360-367.

[7] Bashore T, van der Molen M. Discovery of P300: a tribute. Biol. Psychol 1991; 32: 155-171.

[8] Mertens R, Polich J. P300 from a single-stimulus paradigm: passive *versus* active tasks and stimulus modality. Electroencephalogr. Clin. Neurophysiol.1997; 104: 488-497.

[9] Polich J. Neuropsychology of P3a and P3b:a theoretical overview. In: Moore N, Arikan, K. (Eds.), Brainwaves and Mind:Recent Developments. Kjellberg Press, Wheaton, IL 2004: 15-29.

[10] Jasper HH. The ten-twenty electrode system of the international federation. Electroenc Clin Neurophysiol 1958; 10: 371-5.

[11] Aquino AMCM, Bardão R, Barbosa MM, Colafemina JF, Gonçales AS, Casagrande-Souza VMR. O potencial endógeno nos distúrbios de atenção e memória auditiva. Rev Bras Otorrinolaringol 2000; 66: 225-30.

[12] Pineroli JCA, Campos DS, Wiemes GR, Meneses MS, Mocellin M. Avaliação auditiva central com BERA e P300 na Doença de Parkinson. Rev Bras Otorrinolaringol 2002; 68: 462-6.

[13] Farias LS, Toniolo IF, Cóser PL. P300: avaliação eletrofisiológica da audição em crianças sem e com repetência escolar. R. Bras. Otorrinolaringol 2004; 70: 194-199.

[14] Duarte JL, Alvarenga, KDF, Costa OA. Potencial cognitivo P300 realizado em campo livre. Rev. Bras. Otorrinolaringol 2004; 70: 781-786.

[15] Alvarenga K, Duarte JL, Silva DPC, Agostinho-Pesse RS, Negrato CA, Costa OA. Potencial cognitivo P300 em indivíduos com diabetes mellitus. Rev Bras Otorrinolaringol 2005; 71: 202-7.

[16] Hirayasu Y, Samura M, Ohta H, Ogura C. Sex effects on rate of change of P300 latency with age. Electroencephalogr Clin Neurophysiol 2000; 111: 187-94.

[17] Lin E, Polich J. P300 habituation patterns: individual differences from ultradian rhythms. Percept Mot Skills 1999; 88: 1111-25.

[18] Johnson RJ. On the neural generators of the P300 component of the event-related potential. Psychophysiol 1993; 30: 90-7.

[19] Squires NK, Squires KC, Hillyard SA. Two varieties of long-latency positive waves evoked by unpredicatable autditory stimuli in man. Electroencephalograp Clin Neurophysiol 1975; 39: 387-401.

[20] Snyder E, Hillyard S. Long-latency evoked potentials to irrelevant, deviant stimuli. Behav. Biol 1976; 16: 319-331.

[21] Knight R, Scabini D, Woods D, Clayworth C. Contributions of temporal parietal junction to the human auditory P3. Brain Res 1989; 502: 109-116.

[22] Polich J. Normal variation of P300 from auditory stimuli. Electroencephalogr Clin Neurophysiol 1986; 65: 236-40.

[23] Jeon Y, Polich J. P3a from a passive visual stimulus task. Clin. Neurophysiol 2001; 112: 2202-2208.

[24] Simons R, Graham F, Miles M, Chen X. On the relationship of P3a and the novelty-P3. Biol Psychol 2001; 56: 207-218.

[25] Courchesne E, Kilman B, Galambos R, Lincoln A. Autism: processing of novel auditory information assessed by event-related brain potentials. Electroencephalogr. Clin Neurophysiol 1984; 59: 238-248.

[26] He B, Lian J, Spencer KM. A cortical potential imaging analysis of the P300 and novelty P3 components. Human Brain Mapping 2001; 12: 120-130.

[27] Polich J, Martin S. P300, cognitive capability, and personality: a correlational study of university undergraduates. Pers Individ Differ 1992; 13: 533-543.

[28] Houlihan M, Stelmack R, Campbell K. Intelligence and the effects of perceptual processing demands, task difficulty, and processing speed on P300, reaction time, and movement time. Intelligence 1998; 26: 9-25.

[29] Reinvang I. Cognitive event-related potentials in neuropsychological assessment. Neuropsychol Rev 1999; 9: 231-248.

[30] Oken B. Endogenous event-related potentials. In: Chiappa, K. (Ed.), Evoked Potentials in Clin Medicine. Lippincott-Raven Publishers, NewYork 1997; 529-563.

[31] Sommer W, Leuthold H, Matt J. The expectancies that govern P300 are mostly automatic and unconscious. Behav Brain Sci 1998; 21: 149-150.
[32] Donchin E. Surprise!. Surprise? Psychophysiol 1981; 18: 493-513.
[33] Sokolov E. Brain functions: neuronal mechanisms of learning and memory. Ann Rev Psychol 1977; 28: 85-112.
[34] Ravden D, Polich J. On P300 measurement stability: habituation, intra-trial block variation, and ultradian rhythms. Biol Psychol 1999; 51: 59-76.
[35] Donchin E, Karis D, Bashore T, Coles M, Gratton G. Cognitive Psychophysiol and human information processing. In: Coles M, Donchin E, Porges S. (Eds.), Psychophysiol: Systems, Processes, and Applications. The Guilford Press. New York 1986; 244-267.
[36] Paller K, McCarthy G, Wood C. ERPs predictive of subsequent recall and recognition performance. Biol Psychol 1988; 26: 269-276.
[37] Johnson R. The amplitude of the P300 component of the event-related potentials: review and synthesis. In: Ackles P, Jennings J, Coles, M. (Eds.), Advances in Psychophysiol, JAI Press, Inc., Greenwich CT 1988; 2: 69-137.
[38] McCarthy G, Donchin E. A metric for thought: a comparison of P300 latency and reaction time. Science 1981; 211: 77-80.
[39] Nieuwenhuis S, Aston-Jones G, Cohen J. Decision making, the P3, and the locus coeruleus-norepinephrine system. Psychol Bull 2005; 131: 510-32.
[40] Verleger R, Jas´kowskis P, Wascher E. Evidence for an integrative role of P3b in linking reaction to perception. J Psychophysiol 2005; 19: 150.
[41] Yordanova J, Kolev V, Polich J. P300 and alpha event-related desynchronization (ERD). Psychophysiol 2001; 38: 143-52.
[42] Kok A. On the utility of P3 amplitude as a measure of processing capacity. Psychophysiol 2001; 38: 557-577
[43] Duncan-Johnson CC, Donchin E. On quantifying surprise: The variation in event-related potentials with subjective probability. Psychophysiol 1977; 14: 456-467.
[44] Johnson R, Donchin E. Sequential expectancies and decision-making in a changing environment: an electrophysiological approach. Psychophysiol 1982; 19: 183-200.
[45] Squires KC, Wickens C, Squires NK, Donchin E. Effect of stimulus sequence on waveform of cortical event-related potential. Science 1976; 193: 1142-1146
[46] Isreal JB, Chesney GL, Wickens CD, Donchin E. P300 and tracking difficulty: evidence for multiple resources in dual-task performance. Psychophysiol 1980; 17: 259-273.
[47] Kramer AF, Wickens CD, Donchin E. Processing of stimulus properties: evidence for dual-task integrality. J Exp Psychol Hum Percept Perform 1985; 11: 393-408.
[48] Wickens C, Kramer A, Vanasse L, Donchin E. Performance of concurrent tasks: a psychophysiological analysis of the reciprocity of information-processing resources. Science 1983; 221: 1080-1082.
[49] Kahneman D. Attention and effort. Englewood-Cliffs: Prentice Hall 1973.
[50] Polich J, Howard L, Starr A. P300 latency correlates with digit span. Psychophysiol 1983; 20: 665-669.
[51] Kok A. Internal and external control: a two-factor model of amplitude change of event-related potentials. Biol. Psychol 1990; 74: 203-236.
[52] Polich J, Kok, A. Cognitive and Biol determinants of P300: an integrative review. Biol Psychol 1995; 41: 103-146.
[53] Karis D, Fabiani M, Donchin E. "P300" and memory: Individual differences in the von Restorff effect. Cog Psychol 1984; 16: 117-216.
[54] Fabiani M, Karis D, Donchin E. Effects of mnemonic strategy manipulation in a Von Restorff paradigm. Electroencephalogr Clin Neurophysiol 1990; 75: 2-35
[55] Donchin E, Coles MGH. Is the P300 component a manifestation of context updating? Behav Brain Sciences 1988; 11: 357-374.
[56] Curran T. Effects of attention and confidence on the hypothesized ERP correlates of recollection and familiarity. Neuropsychologia 2004; 42: 1088-1106.
[57] Rushby JA, Barry RJ, Johnstone SS. Event-related potential correlates of serial-position effects during an elaborative memory test. Int J Psychophysiol 2002; 46: 13-27.

[58] Näätänen R. The role of attention in auditory information processing as revealed by event-related potentials and other brain measures of cognitive function. Behav Brain Sciences 1990; 13: 201-288.
[59] Polich J. Meta-analysis of P300 normative aging studies. Psychophysiol 1996; 33: 334-353.
[60] Fjell A, Walhovd K. P300 and neuropsychological tests as measures of aging: scalp topography and cognitive changes. Brain Topogr 2001; 14: 25-40.
[61] Polich J, Ladish C, Bloom FE. P300 assessment of early Alzheimer's disease. Electroencephalogr Clin Neurophysiol 1990; 77: 179-189.
[62] Potter D, Barrett K. Assessment of mild head injury with ERPs and neuropsychological tasks. J Psychophys 1999; 13: 173-189.
[63] Polich J, Corey-Bloom J. Alzheimer's disease and P300: review and evaluation of task and modality. Curr Alzheimer Res 2005; 2: 515-525.
[64] McPherson DL. Late Potentials of the Auditory System. San Diego, California: Singular Publishing Group. Inc 1996.
[65] Hall JW. Handbook of auditory evoked responses. 3nd ed. Massachusetts, Boston: Allyn and Bacon 1990.
[66] Eichele T, Specht K, Moosmann M, Jongsma MLA, Quiroga RQ, Hordby H, Hugdahl K. Assessing the spatiotemporal evolution of neuronal activation with single-trial event-related potentials and functional MRI. Proc Nat Acad Sci 2005; 102: 17798-17803.
[67] Linden D. The P300: where in the brain is it produced and what does it tell us? The Neuroscientist 2005; 6: 563-576.
[68] Soltani M, Knight R. Neural origins of the P300. Crit Rev Neurobiol 2000; 14: 199-224.
[69] Verleger R. Event-related potentials and cognition a critique of the context updating hypothesis and an alternative interpretation of P300. Behav Brain Sci 1988; 11: 343-427.
[70] Halgren E, Squires N, Wilson C, Rohbraugh J, Bab T, Crandall P. Endogenous potentials in the human hippocampal formation and amygdale by infrequent events. Science 1980; 210: 803-805.
[71] McCarthy G, Wood C, Williamson P, Spencer D. Task-dependent field potentials in human hippocampal formation. J Neurosci 1989; 9: 4253-4266.
[72] Smith M, Halgren E. Dissociation of recognition memory components following temporal lobe lesions. J Exp Psychol Gen 1989; 15: 50-60.
[73] Rugg M, Pickles C, Potter D, Roberts R. Normal P300 following extensive damage to the left medial temporal lobe. J Neurol Neurosurg Psychiatry 1991; 54: 217-222.
[74] Onofrj M, Fulgente T, Nobiolio D, Malatesta G, Bazzano S, Colamartino P, Gambi D. P300 recordings in patients with bilateral temporal lobe lesions. Neurology 1992; 42: 1762-1767.
[75] Molnar M. On the origin of the P300 event-related potential component. Int J Psychophysiol 1994; 17: 129-144.
[76] Polich J, Squire L. P300 from amnesic patients with bilateral hippocampal lesions. Electroencephalogr. Clin Neurophysiol 1993; 86: 408-417.
[77] Knight R. Contribution of human hippocampal region to novelty detection. Nature 1996; 383: 256-259.
[78] Nakajima Y, Miyamoto K, Kikuchi M. Estimation of neural generators of cognitive potential P300 by dipole tracing method. No To Shinkei 1994; 46: 1059-1065.
[79] Tarkka IM, Stokic DS, Basile LF, Papanicolaou AC. Electric source localization of the auditory P300 agrees with magnetic source localization. Electroencephalogr Clin Neurophysiol 1995; 96: 538-545.
[80] Pardo J, Fox P, Raichle M. Localization of human system for sustained attention by positron emission tomography. Nature 1991; 349: 61-64.
[81] Posner M. Attention as a cognitive neural system. Curr Dir Psychol Sci 1992; 11: 1-14.
[82] McCarthy G, Luby M, Gore J, Goldman-Rakic P. Infrequent events transiently activate human prefrontal and parietal cortex as measured by functional MRI. J Neurophysiol 1997; 77: 1630-1634.
[83] Verbaten M, Huyben M, Kemner C. Processing capacity and the frontal P3. Int J Psychophysiol 1997; 25: 237-248.
[84] Knight RT. Decreased response to novel stimuli after prefrontal lesions in man. Electroencephalogr Clin Neurophysiol 1984; 59: 9-20.
[85] Knight R, Grabowecky M, Scabini D. Role of human prefrontal cortex in attention control. Adv Neurol 1995; 66: 21-34.

[86] Yamaguchi S, Knight RT. Anterior and posterior association cortex contributions to the somatosensory P300. J Neuroscience 1991; 11: 2039-2054.
[87] Knight R. Neural mechanisms of event-related potentials from human lesion studies. In: Rohbraugh J, Parasuraman R, Johnson R. (Eds.). Event-Related Brain Potentials: Basic Issues and Applications. Oxford University Press, New York 1990; 3-18.
[88] Polich J. Overview of P3a and P3b. In: Polich, J. (Ed.), Detection of Change: Event-Related Potential and fMRI Findings. Kluwer Academic Press, Norwell, MA 2003; 83-98.
[89] Squire L, Kandel E. Memory from mind to molecules. New York: Scientific American Library 1999.
[90] Desimone R, Miller EK, Chelazzi L, Lueschow A. Multiple memory systems in the visual cortex. In: Gazzaniga MS. editor. The cognitive neurosciences. Cambridge: MA: MIT Press 1995; 475-486
[91] Kirino E, Belger A, Goldman-Rakic P, McCarthy G. Prefrontal activation evoked by infrequent target and novel stimuli in a visual target detection task:an event-related functional magnetic resonance study. J Neurosci 2000; 20: 6612-8.
[92] Escera C, Alho K, Winkler I, Naatane R. Neural mechanisms of involuntary attention to acoustic novelty and change. J Cogn Neurosci 1998; 10: 590-604.
[93] Goldstein A, Spencer K, Donchin E. The influence of stimulus deviance and novelty on the P300 and novelty P3. Psychophysiol 2002; 39: 781-790.
[94] Daffner KR, Mesulam MM, Scinto LF. The central role of the prefrontal cortex in directing attention to novel events. Brain 2000; 123: 927-939.
[95] Daffner K, Mesulam M, Holcomb P, *et al.* Disruption of attention to novel events after frontal lobe. injury in humans. J Neurol Neurosurg Psychiatry 2000; 68: 18-24.
[96] Daffner K, Mesulam M, Seinto L, Calvo V, Faust R, Holcomb P. An electrophysiological index of stimulus unfamiliarity. Psychophysiol 2000; 37: 737-747.
[97] Opitz B, Mecklinger A, Friederici AD, von Cramon DY. The functionalneuroanatomy of novelty processing: integrating ERP and fMRI results. CerebCortex. 1999; 4:379-91.
[98] Dien J, Spencer K, Donchin E. Parsing the late positive complex: mental chronometry and the ERP components that inhabit the neighbourhood of the P300. Psychophysiol 2004; 41: 665 -678.
[99] Kiehl KA, Stevens MC, Laurens KR, Pearlson G, Calhoun VD, Liddle PF. An adaptive reflexive processing model of neurocognitive function: supporting evidence from a large scale (n=100) fMRI study of an auditory oddball task. Neuroimage 2005; 25: 899-915.
[100] Yamaguchi S, Knight RT. Effects of temporal-parietal lesions on the somatosensory P3 to lower limb stimulation. Electroencephalogr Clin Neurophysiol 1992; 84: 139-48
[101] Verleger R, Heide W, Butt C, Kompf D. Reduction of P3b in patients with temporo-parietal lesions. Cogn Brain Res 1994; 2: 103-116.
[102] Kiehl K, Laurens K, Duty T, Forster B, Liddle P. Neural sources involved in auditory target detection and novelty processing: an event-related fMRI study. Psychophysiol 2001; 38: 133-142.
[103] Ford J, Sullivan E, Marsh L, White P, Lim K, Pfefferbaum A. The relationship between P300 amplitude and regional gray matter volumes depends on the attentional system engaged. Electroencephalogr Clin Neurophysiol 1994; 90: 214-28.
[104] Bledowski C, Prvulovic D, Hoechstetter K, Scherg M, Wibral M, Goebel R, Linden D. Localizing P300 generators in visual target and distractor processing: a combined event-related potential and functional magnetic resonance imaging study. J Neurosci 2004; 24: 9353-9360.
[105] Dien J, Spencer KM, Donchin E. Localization of the event-related potential novelty response as defined by principal components analysis. Cognitive Brain Research 2003; 17: 637-650.
[106] Alexander J, Bauer L, Kuperman S, *et al.* Hemispheric differences for P300 amplitude from an auditory oddball task. Int J Psychophysiol 1996; 21: 189-196.
[107] Barcelo F, Suwazono S, Knight R. Prefrontal modulation of visual processing in humans. Nat Neurosci 2000; 3: 399-403.
[108] Alexander J, Polich J. P300 differences between sinistrals and dextrals. Cogn Brain Res 1995; 2: 277-282.
[109] Alexander J, Polich J. Handedness and P300 from auditory stimuli. Brain Cogn 1997; 35: 259-270.
[110] Driesen NR, Raz N. The influence of sex, age, and handedness on corpus callosum morphology: A meta-analysis. Psychobiology 1995; 23: 240-247.
[111] Gurrera RJ, O'Donnell BF, Nestor PG, Gainski J, McCarley RW. The P3 auditory event-related brain potential indexes major personality traits. Biol Psychiat 2001; 49: 922-929.

[112] Stelmack RM, Houlihan M. Event-related potentials, personality, and intelligence: concepts, issues, and evidence. In: Saklofske DH, Zaidner M, editors. International handbook of personality and intelligence. New York: Plenum Press: 1994; 349-65.
[113] Brocke B. The multilevel approach in sensation seeking: potentials and findings of a four-level Res program. In: Stelmack, RM., editor. On the psychobiology of personality. Amsterdam: Elsevier 2004; 267-293.
[114] De Pascalis V. On the Psychophysiol of extraversion. In: Stelmack, RM., editor. On the psychobiology of personality. Amsterdam: Elsevier 2004; 297-329.
[115] Ditraglia G, Polich J P300 and introverted/extraverted personality types. Psychophysiol 1991; 28: 177-184.
[116] Iacono WG, Carlson SR, Malone SM, McGue M. P3 event-related potential amplitude and the risk for disinhibitory disorders in adolescent boys. Arch Gen Psychiatry 2002; 59: 750-757.
[117] Iacono WG, Carlson SR, Malone SM, McGue M. Substance use disorders, externalizing psychopathology and P300 event-related potential amplitude. Int J Psychophysiol 2003; 48: 147-178.
[118] Justus AN, Fin PR, Steinmetz JE. P300, disinhibited personality, and early-onset alcohol problems. Alc: Clin Exp Res 2001; 25: 1457-1466.
[119] Hill S, Locke J, Zezza N, Kaplan B, Neiswanger K, Steinhauer S. Genetic association between reduced P300 amplitude and the DRD2 dopamine receptor A1 allele in children at high risk for alcoholism. Biol Psychiatry 1998; 43: 40-51.
[120] Polich J, Criado JR. Neuropsychology and neuropharmacology of P3a and P3b. Int J Psychophysiol 2006; 60: 172-85.
[121] Buckingham R, Beh HC. The effect of stimulus intensity on the P300. In: Proceedings of the Fifth Australian Psychophysiol Conference. Wollongong, Australia 1995.
[122] Duncan-Johnson C, Donchin E. The P300 component of the event-related brain potential as an index of information processing. Biol Psychology 1983; 14: 1-52.
[123] Croft RJ, Gonsalvez CJ, Gabriel C. Target-to-target interval *versus* probability effects on P300 in one- and two-tone tasks. Pscyhophysiology 2003; 40: 322-328.
[124] Coles M, Smid H, Scheffers M, *et al.* Mental chronometry and the study of human information processing. In: Rugg M and Coles M, Eds. Electrophysiology of the Mind. New York: Oxford University Press: 1995; 94-95.
[125] Duncan-Johnson C, Kopell B. The Stroop effect: Brain potentials localize the source of interference. Science 1981; 214: 938-940.
[126] Ilan AB, Polich J. P300 and response time from a manual Stroop task. Clin Neurophysiol 1999; 110: 367-373
[127] Kosmidis MH, Duncan CC, Mirsky AF. Sex differences in seasonal variations in P300. Biol Psychology 1998; 49: 249-268.
[128] Polich J, Herbst K. P300 as a Clin assay: rationale, evaluation, and findings. Int J Psychophysiol 2000; 3: 3-19.
[129] Costa SMB, Costa Filho AO, Cardoso MRA. Os efeitos da idade e sexona latência do P300. Rev Bras Otorrinolaringol 2002; 68: 891-4
[130] Mullis RJ, Holcomb PJ, Diner BC. The effects of aging on the P3 component of the visual event-related potential. Electroencephalogra Clin Neurophysiol 1985; 62: 141-149.
[131] Ohlrich ES, Barnet AB, Weiss IP, Shanks BL. Auditory evoked potential development in early childhood: A longitudinal study. Electroencephalogr Clin Neurophysiol 1978; 44: 411-23.
[132] Franco GM. O Potencial Evocado Cognitivo em adultos Normais. Arq Neuropsiquiatr 2001; 59: 198-200.
[133] Nakamura Y, Nishimoto K, Akamatu M. The effect of jogging on P300 event related potentials. Electromyography and Clin Neurophysiol 1999; 39: 71-74.
[134] Hoffman LD, Polich J. EEG, ERPs and food consumption. Biol Psychology 1998; 48: 139-11
[135] Austin MP, Mitchell P, Goodwin GM. Cognitive deficits in depression: Possible implications for functional neuropathology. Br J Psychiatry 2001; 178: 200-206.
[136] Liotti M, Mayberg HS. The role of functional neuroimaging in the neuropsychology of depression. J Clin and Experimental Neuropsychology 2001; 23: 121-136.
[137] Williams R, Hagerty BM, Cimprich B, Therrien B, Bay E, Hiraki O. Changes in attention and short-term memory in depression. J Psychiatric Res 2002; 34: 227-238.

[138] Ottowitz WE, Dougherty DD, Savage CR. The neural network basis for abnormalities of attention and executive function in major depressive disorder: Implications for application of the medical disease model to psychiatric disorders. Harvard Rev Psychiatry 2002; 10: 86-99.

[139] Whitehouse WG, Turanski WL, Murray LA. Cognitive processing anomalies in depressive mood disorders. Huntington, NY: Nova Science Publishers. In F. Columbus (Ed.), Advances in Psychology Res 2000; pp. 111-125

[140] Williams R, Hagerty BM, Cimprich B, *et al.* Changes in attention and short-term memory in depression. J Psychiatric Res 2000; 34: 227-238.

[141] Lemelin S, Baruch P, Vincent A, Everett J, Vincent P. Distractibility and processing resource deficit in major depression: Evidence for two deficient attentional processing models. J Nerv Mental Dis 1997; 185: 542-548.

[142] MacQueen GM, Tipper SP, Young LT, Joffe RT, Levitt AJ. Impaired distractor inhibition on a selective attention task in unmedicated, depressed subjects. Psychological Med 2000; 30: 557-564

[143] Ottowitz WE, Dougherty DD, Savage CR. The neural network basis for abnormalities of attention and executive function in major depressive disorder: Implications for application of the medical disease model to psychiatric disorders. Harvard Rev Psychiatry 2002; 10: 86-99.

[144] Ilardi SS, Feldman D. The cognitive neuroscience paradigm: A unifying meta-theoretical framework for the science and practice of Clin psychology. J Clin Psychology 2001; 57: 1067-1088.

[145] Blackwood D, Whalley L, Christie J, Blackburn I, St. Clair D, McInnes A. Changes in auditory P3 event-related potential in schizophrenia and depression. Br J Psychiatry 1987; 150: 154-160.

[146] Pfefferbaum A, Wenegrat B, Ford J, Roth WT, Kopell BS. Clin application of the P3 component of event-related potentials: II. Dementia, depression and schizophrenia. Electroencephalogr Clin Neurophysiol 1984; 59: 104-124.

[147] Yanai I, Fujikawa T, Osada M, Yamawaki S, Touhouda Y. Changes in auditory P300 in patients with major depression and silent cerebral infarction. J Affect Disorders 1997; 46: 263-271.

[148] Mathalon DH, Ford JM, Pfefferbaum A. Trait and state aspects of auditory P300 amplitude reduction in schizophrenia: A longitudinal study. Biol Psychiatry 2000; 47: 434-49.

[149] Ancy J, Gangadhar BN, Janakiramaiah N. deg. Normal'' P300 amplitude predicts rapid response to ECT in melancholia. J Affect Disorders 1996; 41: 211-215.

[150] Murthy P JNV, Gangadhar BN, Janakiramaiah N, Subbakrishna DK. Normalization of P300 amplitude following treatment in dysthymia. Biol Psychiatry 1997; 42: 740-743.

[151] Yanai I, Fujikawa T, Osada M, Yamawaki S, Touhouda Y. Changes in auditory P300 in patients with major depression and silent cerebral infarction. J Affect Disorders 1997; 46: 263-271.

[152] Diner BC, Holcomb PJ, Dykman RA. P300 in major depressive disorder. Psychiatry Res 1985; 15: 175-184.

[153] Pierson A, Ragot R, Van Hooff J, Partiot A, Renault B, Jouvent R. Heterogeneity of information-processing alterations according to dimensions of depression: An event-related potentials study. Biol Psychiatry 1996; 40: 98-115.

[154] Bruder GE, Towey JP, Stewart JW, Friedman D, Tenke C, Quitkin FM. Event related potentials in depression: Influence of task, stimulus hemifield and Clin features on P3 latency. Biol Psychiatry 1991; 30: 233-246.

[155] Kayser J, Bruder GE, Tenke CE, Stewart JW, Quitken FM. Event-related potentials (ERPs) to hemifield presentations of emotional stimuli: Differences between depressed patients and healthy adults in P3 amplitude and asymmetry. Int J Psychophysiol 2002; 36: 211-236.

[156] Grant Sara, Evian Gordon, Claudia Kraiuhin, Steven Coyle, Alan Howson, Russell Meares. The P300 ERP component: an index of cognitive dysfunction xin depression? 1994; 31: 29-38.

[157] Ohira H. Assessibility of negative constructs in depression: An event-related brain potential and reaction time analysis. Jap J Exp Soc Psychol 1996; 35: 304-316.

[158] Ilardi SS, Atchley RA, Enloe A, Kwasny K, Garratt G. Disentangling attentional biases and attentional deficits in depression: An event-related potential P300 analysis. Cognitive Therapy and Res 2007; 31: 175-187.

[159] Coyne JC. Toward an interactional description of depression. Psychiatry 1976; 39: 28-40.

[160] Gordon E, Kraiuhin C, Harris A, Meares R, Howson A. The differential diagnosis of dementia using P3 latency. Biol Psychiatry 1986; 21: 1123-32.

[161] Patterson JV, Michalewski HJ, Starr A. latency variability of the components of auditory ERP to infrequent stimuli. Electroencephalogr Clin Neurophysiol 1988; 71: 45&60

[162] Khanna S, Mukundan R, Channabasavanna SM. Bereits chafts potential in melancholic depression. Biol Psychiatry 1989; 26: 52,9

[163] Himani, OP. Tandon, MS Bhatia. A study of p300-event related evoked potential in the patients of major depression. Indian J Physiol Pharmacol 1999; 43: 367-372.

[164] Kraiuhin C, Gordon E. Covle S *et al.* Normal latency of the P300 evant-related potential in mild-to-moderate Alzheimer's disease and depression. Biol Psychiatry 1990; 28: 372-86

[165] R Singh, R Shukla, PK Dalal, PK Sinha, JK Trivedi. P 300 event related potential in depression. Indian J Psychiatry 2000; 42: 402-409.

[166] M Urretavizcaya, I Moreno, L Benlloch, *et al.* Auditory event-related potentials in 50 melancholic patients: increased N100, N200 and P300 latencies and diminished P300 amplitude. Affect Disord 2003; 74: 293-297.

[167] Fatih Karaaslan, Ali Saffet Gonul, Aslan Oguz, Erdogan Erdinc, Ertugrul Esel. P300 changes in major depressive disorders with and without psychotic features 2003; 73: 283-287.

[168] Jaworska N, Somma E D, Blondeau C, *et al.* Auditory P3 in antidepressant P pharmacotherapy treatment responders, non-responders and controls. Eue Neuro-psychopharma Cop 2013; 23: 1561-1569.

[169] Vandoolaeghe E, van Hunsel F, Nuyten D, Maes M. Auditory event related potentials in major depression: prolonged P300 latency and increased P200 amplitude. J Affect Disord 1998; 48: 105-13.

[170] Murthy P.J. N, Gangadhar B.N., Janakiramaiah N., Subbakrishna D.K. Normalization of P300 amplitude following treatment in dysthymia. Biol Chemistry 1997; 42: 740-743.

Chapter 3: The Impact of Aging on Post-Stroke Depression

CHAPTER 3

The Impact of Aging on Post-Stroke Depression

Ana-Maria Buga[1,2], Madalina Filfan[2,3], Badescu M. George[3] and Aurel Popa-Wagner[1,*]

[1]Department of Psychiatry and Psychotherapy University of Medicine Rostock, Rostock, Germany; [2]Center of Clinical and Experimental Medicine, University of Medicine and Pharmacy Craiova, Romania and [3]Clinic of Psychotherapy, University of Medicine and Pharmacy Craiova, Craiova, Romania

Abstract: Post-stroke depression (PSD) affects about one-third of the ischemic stroke survivors and it is one of the world's most significant health problems. Vascular dysregulation is often met in late-life depression (LLD) and cerebral blood flow (CBF) reduction can influence regional brain functions, contributing to affective and cognitive symptoms. However, it is not clear if perfusion deficits can cause secondary degenerative changes in the brain or that ongoing degenerative changes of the aged brain will be simply aggravated by stroke. A brain injury is accompanied by an exaggerated neuroinflammation by activation of immune-reactive microglial population and is considered a trigger mechanism for depressive-like behavior after injury that may last for weeks or months after stroke and is precipitated by advanced age. Research using animal models and clinical studies of mood disorders highlighted that an increased level of proinflammatory molecules and increased levels of reactive oxygen species (ROS) along with alteration of 5-hydroxy-tryptamine system (5-HT) are associated with decreased neurogenesis. Treatment of PSD includes psychotherapy (CBT-cognitive behavioral therapy) and selective serotonin reuptake inhibitor (SSRI) and selective norepinephrine reuptake inhibitor (SNRI) drugs. More recently, transcranial magnetic stimulation (TMS) has been used to treat depressive patients. Its efficacy is however, questionable. More basic and clinical research is needed to uncover mechanisms underlying depressive behaviour in the elderly caused by perfusion deficits or brain lesioning.

Keywords: Aging, cognitive behavioral therapy (CBT), depression, late-life depression, Major depressive disorder, neuroinflammation, oxidative stress, post stroke depression, psychotherapy, SSRI, transcranial magnetic stimulation (TMS).

INTRODUCTION

Aging, a normal and inevitable process, has an important effect over mind and body. Cardio-vascular problems affect several organs, including brain and may

***Corresponding author Aurel Popa-Wagner:** Department of Psychiatry, Aging & Psychiatric Disorders Group, Rostock University Medical School, Gehlsheimer Straβe 20, D-18147 Rostock, Germany; Tel: +49-381-494-9686; Fax: +49-381-494-9639; E-mail: aurel.popa-wagner@med.uni-rostock.de

Puneetpal Singh and Sarabjit Mastana (Eds)

lead to the development of several psychiatric disorders. Stroke and depression have an increased incidence in elderly with the growth of aged population, there is a common interest in prevention and preserving health of the elderly.

Major depressive disorder (MDD) is a chronic psychiatric disease associated with significant morbidity and mortality. About 1 in 6 individuals will succumb to clinical depression during their lifetime. Several studies have confirmed that in one given year, between 1% and 2% of the individuals over 65 years-old meet the criteria for MDD. It may also complicate the prognosis of other associated chronic diseases. Although there are lots of new discoveries in depression treatment, about one-third of the patients fail to respond to conventional antidepressant medication.

Post-stroke depression (PSD) affects about one-third of the ischemic stroke survivors and is one of the world's most significant health problems. The symptoms related to post-stroke depression are fatigue: insomnia and psychomotor retardation. Aphasia (disturbance in the comprehension and expression of language caused by brain dysfunction) can, in addition, make the post-stroke depression difficult to diagnose.

EPIDEMIOLOGY AND CLINICAL IMPACT OF POST-STROKE DEPRESSION

MDD is a severe psychiatric illness characterized by anhedonia, depressed mood, insomnia or hypersomnia, fatigue or loss of energy, psychomotor agitation or retardation, feelings of guilt or worthlessness, diminished ability to think or focus and recurrent thoughts of death. These symptoms appear nearly every day, during the same period of two weeks, according to diagnostic and statistical manual of mental disorders (DSM-V). Other signs of depression might be feeling irritable, hopeless, helpless, guilty, feeling tired, aches and pain, headaches, cramps or digestive problems which are not calmed down by treatment. The disease has different risk factors like neuroticism, adverse childhood experiences and genetic factors. There is a risk for potential suicide all times during major depressive episodes. Women have a higher risk for suicide attempts but a lower risk to commit suicide in MDD. Men and lonely individuals with a persistent feeling of hopelessness have higher risks of committing suicide.

Depression may be a serious consequence of stroke. World Health Organization data show that stroke is the most common, severe neurological disorder and the the third cause of mortality in adults. Worldwide there are about 15 million people suffering annually from stroke [1].

PSD is among the most frequent neuropsychiatric consequences of stroke. It is estimated that 30% of stroke survivors are also affected by PSD, affecting both short-term recovery and long-term rehabilitation. PSD is associated with poor social recovery (may delay recovery by two years), poor social outcomes, reduced quality of life, reduced rehabilitation treatment efficiency, increased cognitive impairment and mortality [2]. The ageing brain itself may be at risk for depression due to lower amount of neurotransmitters. Stroke may cause depression by modifying the neurotransmitter's metabolism. Studies have confirmed that death risk is three times higher in post-stroke depressed patients than in post-stroke patients without depression [3]. A link between PSD and macrovascular lesions in different areas of the brain (left frontal lobe, bilateral prefrontal cortex, left anterior and right occipital cortex) has been proved in some studies but this association is still under debate [4]. Peak prevalence of MDD occurs in the first 3-6 months after the stroke [5] and this risk appears to remain high after 1-3 years of stroke. PSD prevalence reaches 25-79%, if all depressive episodes in the acute and later post stroke periods are considered [5]. In another study, Robinson and colleagues [6] characterized the natural course of MDD with spontaneous remission typically 1 to 2 years after stroke. Minor depression appeared to be more variable, with both long term and short term depression occurring in these patients. DSM-V diagnostic criteria classify PSD in the group of "mood disorders due to stroke with depressive features". There are studies about differences between PSD and age-associated depression emphasizing that early-onset PSD is characterized by anxiety, loss of libido and feeling of guilt, while later-onset PSD is associated with social isolation and mood variations [7].

COURSE OF PSD

About 40% of patients with PSD develop symptoms within three months after stroke. 30% of non-depressed patients become depressed upon discharge from the hospital. At 6 months after stroke, a majority of patients with PSD continued to have symptoms of depression. The course of depression is different while developing minor depression. Depressed stroke survivors are less likely to comply with their treatment, more irritable and have changes in their personality which is oftenly caused by the physical handicap and daily living limitations [8].

RISK FACTORS FOR PSD

There are multiple factors associated with PSD which includes age, gender, lesion location, stroke severity, psychiatric history, existence of a prior stroke and relationship status.

Older patients may accept the deficits as part of their life whereas younger patients are severely affected as they feel that an important part of their healthy life was stolen [9].

A major component of mechanisms underlying PSD is directly related to the ischemic insult and strongly involve neural circuits that are involved in mood regulation (*e.g.* catecholamine pathway). Since relationship between inflammatory molecules, oxidative stress and neurotropic factors are the major regulatory mechanisms controlling brain plasticity, alteration of these systems forms the molecular basis of cerebral diseases including depression. One of the most important factors involved in PSD in aged subjects is age-related microglial activation in response to stroke. After a brain injury a depressive like symptoms may evolve as a consequence of exaggerated neuro-inflammation due to activation of immune-reactive microglial populations. These symptoms may last for weeks or months after stroke [10].

POST-STROKE DEPRESSION AND MORTALITY

Patients with either major or minor PSD are 3.4 times more likely to die during a 10-year period post-stroke than non-depressed patients. The situation is even worse for patients with PSD having lesser social contacts. Morris *et al.* [2] have observed 90% mortality after stroke in such cases.

IMPACT OF PSD IN AGING POPULATION

Human population is aging at an unprecedented rate. In the year 2000, 10% of the world's population was over 60 years old. It is estimated that in the year 2050, that number will reach to 21%. Older age is associated with higher susceptibility to stroke and poor recovery from brain injury. Depression is also a highly significant problem in elderly and is often associated with cognitive impairments especially after stroke. With a growing aged population, it is important to keep them healthy and to provide them the best possible rehabilitation services after different diseases which affect them.

MOLECULAR AND CELLULAR MECHANISMS OF POST-STROKE DEPRESSION IN AGING BRAIN

Recent studies showed that in ageing brain, ischemic stroke could induce cellular and molecular stimuli in order to activate the repair and maintenance mechanisms. These studies have shown that the repair mechanisms respond different in young and old individuals and are influenced by age-related risks factors. Our study has shown that the ageing human brain has a residual capacity of plasticity [11]. However, the interaction between depression and stroke at the molecular level is still under debate. Several studies suggest that PSD is a consequence of brain lesions that are associated with alteration in synaptic transmission, signaling pathways and aged brain [6, 12-14]. We belive that PSD is a multifactorial disease with two major contributors, biological and psychological.

A question arises whether cerebral ischemia causes secondary degenerative changes in the brain or whether ongoing degenerative changes of the aged brain will be simply aggravated by stroke. From a psychological perspective, the incidence and severity of PSD is determined not only by individual differences in emotional reactions to disease (*e.g.* negative attitude) but also by the severity of physical and cognitive impairment [15, 16].

Recent studies have shown the age-specific response to cerebral ischemia at molecular level. Many genes are involved in DNA repair, while some other genes are involved in neurotransmission and are associated with dopamine, serotonin and gamma-aminobutyric acid (GABA) signaling pathways. Several genes are involved in cognitive processes as well (cortistatin - *CORT*, dopamine receptor-*DRD1*, dopamine receptor D2-*DRD2*, GABA receptor-*GABAD*, and G protein-coupled receptor 88- *GPR88*, *ACVR1C*, *HTR2B* and *PNOC*), behavioral trait (*CORT*, *DRD2*, *GABAD*, protein phosphatase 1, regulatory subunit 1B - *PPP1R1B*, regulator of G-protein signaling 9-*RGS9*, *GPR88*, and RASD family member 2-*RASD2*), sleep (*CORT*), drug abuse (*DRD2*, *GABAD*, *PPP1R1B* and *RGS9*), and pain regulation (*CORT*, *GABAD*, indoleamine 2,3-dioxygenase 1-*IDO1*, *RASD2*, and *RGS9*). Studies have shown that there is a disregulated response in aged brain after stroke which suggest that the aged brain can initiate and maintain the neurotransmission-associated signaling pathway [11, 17, 18].

Results from animal model and clinical studies of mood disorders highlighted that the increased proinflammatory molecules, increased reactive oxygen species (ROS) and alteration of 5-hydroxy-tryptamine system (5-HT) are associated with decreased neurogenesis. Cerebral ischemia as well as aging process itself contribute to these changes. All these factors are interconnected in a vicious cycle (Fig. **1**).

Clinical studies have shown that the impaired adult neurogenesis and abnormal synaptic integration of newly born neurons are key processes associated not only with mood disorders but also with cerebral ischemia. In the depressed older adults, subjective complaints of poor memory and lack of concentration are quite common [19]. One possible mechanism of impaired cognition is to decreased neurogenesis due to ageing. Indeed, hippocampal neurogenesis has been shown to decrease steadily with aging [20]. Since aged animals might be prone both to develop a depressive phenotype [21] and cerebral ischemia [22], more severe PSD symptoms in aged organisms can be expected.

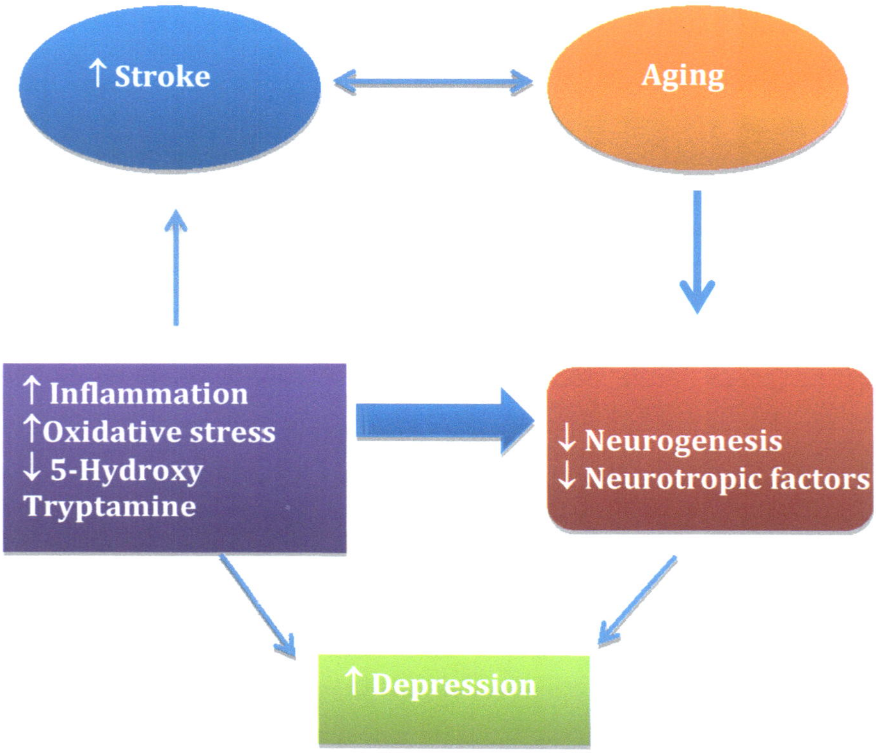

Fig. (1). Molecular processes associated with PSD.

Several neurotransmitters are modified in MDD. The brain uses different chemical substances to communicate within the nervous system. Decreased levels of norepinephrine and serotonin are thought to be the most important and may be the one factor involved associated with MDD. Recent data suggest that in mood disorders, regional reduction in the levels of norepinephrine and serotonin central nervous system may appear probably caused by a reduction in number and or size of glia and neurons. Other researchers consider that alteration of neuronal plasticity may be one reason for the mood disorders. That is why MDD, which was previously considered to be strictly a neurochemical disorder, is now considered to be caused by changes in neuronal plasticity and disturbances in neurotransmission.

Until now scientists have examined several genes which may predispose the individual to depression. These genes control the metabolism of neurotransmitters and their receptors. In this regard, the serotonin transporter gene (SERT) is one which concerns the scientists and has been studied extensively. The most significant polymorphism is HTTLPR (hydroxyl tryptamine linked polymorphic region) which is in the promoter region and has two alleles (short and long). The short allele slows down the serotonin transporter synthesis whereby the serotonin neurons adapt slowly to the changes in their stimulation. When an acute stressor increases serotonin release, this polymorphism may influence person's mood.

Brain-derived neurotrophic factor (BDNF) is a growth factor that helps in the survival of adult neurons, growth and differentiation of new neurons and synapses. BDNF acts on neurons from central and peripheral nervous system. This factor also stimulates the transcription of genes involved in serotonin synthesis. BDNF is coded by a gene with 2 alleles encoding for "Met" and "Val". The presence of "Met" allele is associated with a relatively small hippocampus at birth which may be render the carrier to stress hypersensitivity.

In postmortem studies, lower amounts of BDNF have been found in the hippocampus and prefrontal cortex of the symptomatic depressed patient, which is evident in living depressed patients also. BDNF is an attractive candidate to explain the complex interaction between depression, antidepressants and post stroke recovery. BDNF protects against ischemic brain injury and attenuates apoptosis in cultured neurons after glucose deprivation. In addition, BDNF signaling is crucially involved in hippocampal neurogenesis. In pre-infarct cortex, this factor improves functional recovery after stroke whereas intra-ventricular administration of BDNF antisense oligonucleotides impedes re-learning of a motor skill in a focal ischemia [23].

Hypothalamic-pituitary-adrenal (HPA) axis is activated by stress which activates the release of corticotropin releasing factor (direct method). There is also an indirect method of activation of the HPA axis by releasing corticotropin- releasing factor from other part of the brain (*e.g.* amygdala). This chain reaction explains that why depressive patients have increased levels of norepinephrine in blood plasma and cerebrospinal fluid. Dopamine is another neurotransmitter which is supposed to have an important role in major depressive disorder. When amygdala senses an environmental stressor, it increases the dopamine level from the prefrontal cortex and ventral striatum. A local inhibitory feedback appears which ensures homeostasis. Problem worsens when stress factor is severe and the feedback is disrupted by abnormal levels of striatal BDNF. That abnormal feedback explains why depressed patients often suffer from anhedonia (lack of pleasure) [24].

There are two main theories for PSD; the neurotransmitter and cytokine hypotheses It has been postulated that ischemic lesions may interrupt the biogenic amine-containing axons ascending from the brainstem to the cerebral cortex leading to a decreased availability of biogenic amines in limbic structures of frontal and temporal lobes as well as in basal ganglia. Ischemic lesions interrupt the projections ascending from midbrain and brainstem, leading to a decreased bioavailability of the biogenic amines serotonin (5HT), dopamine (DA) and norepinephrine (NE). Acetylcholine may also be involved [23]. However, stroke and brain injury leave the patient vulnerable to neuropsychiatric and neurocognitive symptoms [10, 25].

INFLAMMATION AND NEUROINFLAMMATION

It is already known that there is an association between MDD and increased levels of inflammatory markers. In one third of the depressed patients, elevated levels of inflammatory biomarkers including interleukin-6 (IL-6), IL-8, interferon-alpha (IFN-α), Tumor necrosis factor-alpha (TNF-α) and acute phase reactant protein have been found. Once the patients start responding to the antidepressant treatment, the levels of inflammatory markers begin to normalize [26-29]. Studies confirmed that there is a significant linear relationship between increased levels of IL-6, IL-8 and depressive symptoms at baseline and after a 2 year follow-up [28]. It was suggested that IL-1β and interleukin 1 receptor antagonist (IL1ra) are significantly associated with depression in elderly [30, 31]. IFN-α has also been associated frequently with significant psychiatric morbidity especially major depression in almost 45% of patients [32-34]. In obese women, inflammation is associated with elevated concentrations of inflammatory markers- IL-6, C-reactive protein (CRP) and adipokines which are correlated with increased symptoms of anxiety and depression [35]. After surgical removal of fat in obese, the inflammatory markers are reduced resulting in reduced inflammation [36]. A systemic inflammation allows the pro-inflammatory cytokines to access the central nervous system which interfere with serotonin metabolism, synaptic plasticity and hippocampal neurogenesis [37, 38]. These modifications lead to behavioral consequences which include depression [35]. It is also evident that the patients treated with cytokines for other diseases also have an increased risk to develop MDD [39]. Intraperitoneal administration of TNF-α in animal model (mice) has been observed to induce depressive behavior [40].

MICROGLIA, SYNAPTIC PLASTICITY AND DEPRESSIVE BEHAVIOR

While aging, an overexpression of pro-inflammatory factors including cytokines appears [41, 42]. In brain, these changes appear at first by chronic activation of perivascular and parenchymal macrophages/microglia expressing pro-inflammatory cytokines and increased number of astrocytes [43-45]. The neuro-inflammation is different from classic inflammation, but may stimulate neurodegenerative and psycopathological events by inflammation-like glial response. In consequence microglias are recognized as components of an intrinsic brain immune system [46]. In different studies ketamine-NMDA receptor antagonist was used in depressed patients [47, 48]. In animal models ketamine's antidepressant effect was mediated by increased synaptic signaling proteins and increased number of new synapses in prefrontal cortex [49, 50]. In a postmortem study of patients who had suffered from MDD, the signaling mammalian target of repamycin (mTOR) was deficient in the prefrontal cortex [51]. In other postmortem studies, a significant reduction in depressed patients' prefrontal cortex induces the expression of postsynaptic proteins involved in glutamate neurotransmission including NMDA receptor subunits (NR2A, NR2B), metabotropic glutamate receptor subtype 5 (mGluR5) and postsynaptic density 95kDa (PSD-95) [52, 53]. A reduction of mTOR and mTOR-dependent translation pathway (p70S6K, eIF4B, and p-eIF4B) was observed in a recent study which compared MDD patients with psychiatrically healthy controls [54]. The mTOR pathway has different physiological functions. In brain it is involved in several forms of long lasting synaptic plasticity and long term memory [55]. Synaptic plasticity is described as the possibility of the synaptic network to adapt to internal and external stimuli and it is very important for learning and memory, for brain function, recovery after injuries, especially in a young and healthy brain. The problem is that neuroplasticity decreases with age due to alterations in gene expression, dendritic morphology, cellular connectivity and Ca2+ dysregulation [11, 56, 57].

Alluding to this, one may consider that deficits in mTOR pathway contribute to depression pathogenesis [54]. Microglia *via* complement receptor 3 (CR3) is considered to have an impact over the synaptic remodeling and plasticity in the healthy brain [58-63]. CR3 is expressed on microglia surface and complement component 3 (CC3). Disruption of CR3/CC3 signaling is specific to microglia in the CNS and resulted in sustained deficits in brain wiring and structural remodeling [63]. It appears to be a connection between microglia, neuroplasticity, inflammation and mood regulation. After stroke, microglia move toward the injured area where they engulf and clear the damaged cellular debris [59, 64, 65].

PERFUSION DEFICITS IN THE ELDERLY AND INFLAMMATION

With ageing, there is a reduction in cerebral blood flow due to hardened large arteries or lumina occlusion in small arterioles which may lead to a form of depression which is called "vascular depression" [66]. Perfusion deficit in elderly leads to microglial activation and neuroinflammation [67, 68], which causes demyelination and neurodegeneration [69]. Studies on animal model confirmed that aging and preclinical neurodegenerative disease processes in old subjects are followed by development of a prime and immune reactive population of microglia [70-75]. Intracerebral vessel occlusion is strongly dependent on age and age specific changes are associated with cerebral ischemia (Fig. **2**).

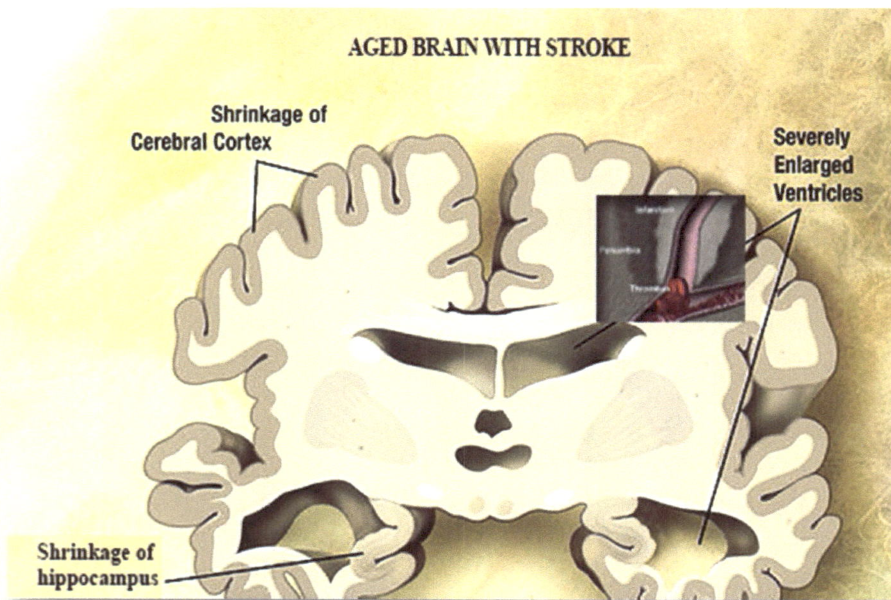

Fig. (2). Aged brain with stroke.

On the other hand, immune activation may be a characteristic of depression [76, 77] and may precipitate depressive symptoms [34, 78]. All these arguments prove that there is a connection between inflammatory process, multiple neurodegenerative pathways, pro-inflammatory cytokines and depression [79]. Inflammation may be associated both with depression and dementia [38, 80-82]. In age-related perfusion deficit there is a microglia activation which may contribute to affective and cognitive symptoms noticed in late-life depression (Fig. **3**). Vascular dysregulation is often present in LLD (late-life depression) and cerebral blood flow (CBF) reduction can influence regional brain functions contributing to affective and cognitive symptoms [83-85]. The subcortical white matter is very susceptible to infarction because of CBF reduction [86] and impaired auto-regulation [87]. Further research on neuroinflammation may expose novel biomarkers and treatment targets.

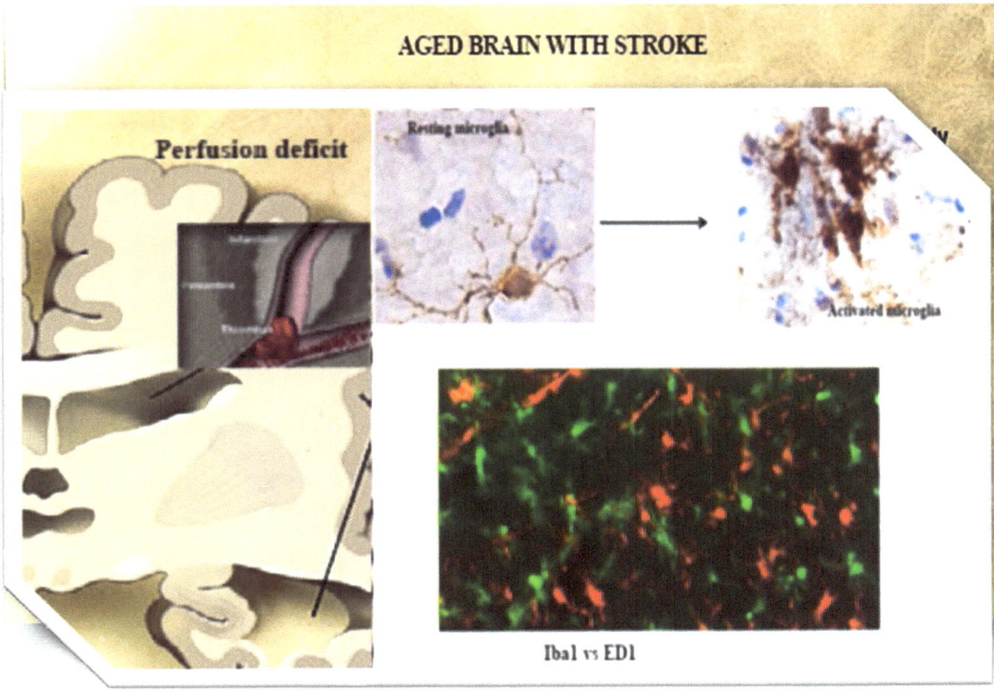

Fig. (3). Age-related deficit and microglial activation after stroke.

SCREENING INSTRUMENTS IN POST STROKE DEPRESSION

Diagnosis of post stroke depression may be difficult due to aphasia and other cognitive deficits, therefore different diagnostic instruments are regularly used in screening. There are multiple scales used to diagnose PSD; Beck Depression Inventory, Hamilton Rating Scale for Depression, Visual Analogue Mood Scale, Clinical Global Impression of the nursing and study personnel, Diagnostic and statistical manual of mental disorders (DSM-V).

There are many studies aimed at optimizing these scales [88]. It has been concluded that none of these diagnostic or screening instruments stood apart from another, use of Visual Analogue Mood Scale in post stroke patients with aphasia or other cognitive impairments is not recommended [88]. Other studies consider that PSDRS (Post stroke Depression Rating Scale) has a better performance than HAM-D (Hamilton Depression Rating Scale) in post stroke patients and is an useful instrument of diagnosis in clinical practice [89].

THERAPEUTIC TARGETS IN POST STROKE DEPRESSION TREATMENT

Presently, the treatment of PSD is done by psychotherapy (CBT-cognitive behavioral therapy), selective serotonin reuptake inhibitors (SSRIs) especially citalopram, fluoxetine and sertraline, serotonin and norepinephrine reuptake inhibitor (SNRI), especially duloxetine and venlafaxine (National Institute of Mental Health- Depression and stroke). Citalopram is the single most widely studied antidepressant agent in PSD. Secondly, transcranial magnetic stimulation (TMS) one of the non-invasive forms of brain stimulation is oftenly used to treat neuropsychiatric illnesses. This therapy was developed for the treatment of Alzheimer's disease, post-stroke recovery and depression in elderly. US federal drug agency (FDA) already approves TMS for treating MDD and it is promising also for bipolar disorder, schizophrenia, obsessive-compulsive disorder and some other diseases [90].

The TMS device spreads short current pulses through a stimulating coil positioned on the patient's head so that the neurons in a focal region are stimulated. However, the effect is not entirely local because the neurons transmit their activity trans-synaptically to connect subcortical and transcortical regions. The stimulation effects depend on the frequency of stimulation. The treatment for MDD consists of 10 hertz TMS sessions applied to the left dorsolateral prefrontal cortex for 6 weeks. TMS may be sometimes preferred as an antidepressant strategy compared to antidepressant medication which sometimes causes different complications. Studies observed that young depressed patients responded better to TMS than elderly patients for the same treatment [90]. Some studies emphasize that TMS has no antidepressant effect in elderly [91-93] whereas, other studies concluded that age is a confounding factor in this kind of therapy [94] and some studies consider that it has only a modest antidepressant effect in elderly [95]. An explanation worth considering is that in elderly the distance between scalp-to-cortex increases because of the motor and prefrontal cortex atrophy [90, 96].

Brain atrophy in elderly may also influence the delivered dosage of magnetic stimulation by reducing it.

Treatment-resistant depression (TRD) is a term used in clinical psychiatry to describe cases of major depressive disorder (MDD) that do not respond adequately to adequate courses of at least two antidepressants. It is associated with high levels of circulating hs-CRP whereby patients respond better to infliximab, a monoclonal antibody against TNF-α [97]. An increased level of CRP was also observed following an acute stroke, as well as in normal aging. It has been shown that different pathophysiological roles of high circulating CRP concentrations are evident in acute stroke [98]. Where all these conditions are interrelated and interacted with each other remain to be elucidated.

CONFLICT OF INTERESTS

The authors confirm that this chapter contents have no conflict of interest.

ACKNOWLEDGEMENTS

This research was supported by UEFISCDI Grant no PNII-ID-FL-2011-2 (to AMB) and Grants no PN-II-ID-PCE-2011-3-0848 and and PCCA nr 80/2012 (to APW).

REFERENCES

[1] WHO. Recommendations on stroke prevention, diagnosis, and therapy. Report of the WHO Task Force on Stroke and other Cerebrovascular Disorders. Stroke1989; 20: 1407-31.

[2] Morris P, Robinson R, Andrzejewski P, Samuels J, Price T. Association of depression with 10-year poststroke mortality. Am J Psychiatry 1993; 150: 124-129.

[3] Whyte EM, Mulsant BH. Post stroke depression: epidemiology, pathophysiology,and biological treatment. Biol Psychiatry 2002; 52: 253-64.

[4] Everson SA, Roberts RE, Goldberg DE, Kaplan GA. Depressive symptoms and increased risk of stroke mortality over a 29-year period. Arch Intern Med 1998; 259: 1133-8.

[5] Provinciali L, Coccia M. Post-stroke and vascular depression: a critical review. Neurol Sci 2002; 22: 417-28.

[6] Robinson RG: The clinical neuropsychiatry of stroke. Cambridge (MA): Cambridge University Press. 2006.

[7] Paradiso S, Ohkubo T, Robinson RG. Vegetative and psychological symptoms associated with depressed mood over the first two years after stroke. Int J Psychiatry Med 1997; 27: 137-57.

[8] Pohjasvaara T1, Leppävuori A, Siira I, Vataja R, Kaste M, Erkinjuntti T. Frequency and clinical determinants of poststroke depression. Stroke 1998; 29: 2311-7.

[9] Rusin M. Stroke Rehabilitation. A geropsychological perspective. Arch Phys Med Rehabil 1990; 71: 914-922.

[10] Fenn AM, Gensel JC, Huang Y, Popovich PG, Lifshitz J,Godbout JP. Immune activation promotes depression 1 month after diffuse brain injury: a role for primed microglia. Biol Psychiatry biopsych. 2013.

[11] Buga AM, Scholz CJ, Kumar S,*et al.* Identification of new therapeutic targets by genome-wide analysis of gene expression in the ipsilateral cortex of aged rats after stroke. PLoS ONE 2012; 7: 12.

[12] Kim JT, Park MS, Yoon GJ, *et al.* White matter hyperintensity as a factor associated with delayed mood disorders in patients with acute ischemic stroke. Eur Neurol 2011; 66: 343-349.

[13] Narushima K, Kosier JT, Robinson RG. A reappraisal of poststroke depression, intra- and interhemispheric lesion location using metaanalysis. J Neuropsychiatry Clin Neurosc 2003; 15: 422- 430.

[14] Kohen R, Cain KC, Mitchell PH, *et al.* Association of serotonin transporter gene polymorphisms with poststroke depression. Arch Gen Psychiatry 2008; 65: 1296-1302.

[15] Stuller KA, Jarrett B, DeVries AC. Stress and social isolation increase vulnerability to stroke. Exp Neurol 2012; 233: 33-39.

[16] Kouwenhoven SE, Kirkevold M, Engedal K, Biong S, Kim HS. The lived experience of stroke survivors with early depressive symptoms: Alongitudinal perspective. Int J Qual Stud Health Well- being 2011; 6.

[17] Sieber MW, Guenther M, Jaenisch N. Age-specific transcriptional response to stroke. Neurobiol Aging 2014; 35: 1744-54.

[18] Creutzfeldt, C.J., Holloway, R.G., Walker, M. Symptomatic and palliative care Cunningham C, Wilcockson DC, Campion S, Lunnon K, Perry VH (2005) Central and systemic endotoxin challenges exacerbate the local inflammatory response and increase neuronal death during chronic neurodegeneration. J Neurosci 2012; 25: 9275-9284

[19] Christensen H, Jorm A, Mackinnon A, *et al.* Age differences in depression and anxiety symptoms: a structural equation modelling analysis of data from a general population sample. Psychol Med 1999; 29: 325-339.

[20] Couillard-Despres S, Vreys R, Aigner L, Van der Linden A. *In vivo* monitoring of adult neurogenesis in health and disease. Front Neurosci 2011; 5: 67.

[21] Huston JP, Schulz D. Toward an animal model of extinctioninduced despair: focus on aging and physiological indices. J Neural Transm 2009; 116: 1029-1036.

[22] Baltan S. Ischemic injury to white matter: an age-dependent process. Neuroscientist 2009; 15: 126- 133.

[23] Popa-Wagner A, Buga AM, Tica AA, Albu CV. Perfusion deficits, inflammation and aging precipitate depressive behavior, Biogerontology 2014; 15(5): 439-48.

[24] Nestler EJ, Carlezon WA Jr. The mesolimbic dopamine reward circuit in depression. Biol Psychiatry 2006; 59: 1151-9

[25] Dimopoulos N, Piperi C *et al.* Increased plasma levels of 8-iso-PGF2alpha and IL-6 in an elderly population with depression. Psychiatry Res 2008; 16: 59-66

[26] Alexopoulos GS. The vascular depression hypothesis: 10 years later. Biol Psychiatry 2006; 60: 1304-1305.

[27] Miller AH, Maletic V, Raison CL. Inflammation and its discontents: the role of cytokines in the pathophysiology of major depression. Biol Psychiatry 2009; 65: 732-741.

[28] Baune BT, Stuart M, Gilmour A, *et al.* The relationship between subtypes of depression and cardiovascular disease: a systematic review of biological models. Transl Psychiatry 2012; 13(2): c92.

[29] Papakostas GI, Shelton RC, Kinrys G, *et al.* Assessment of a multi-assay, serum-based biological diagnostic test for major depressive disorder: a pilot and replication study. Mol Psychiatry 2013; 18: 332-339.

[30] van den Biggelaar AH, Gussekloo J, *et al.* Inflammation and interleukin-1 signaling network contribute to depressive symptoms but not cognitive decline in old age. Exp Gerontol 2007; 42: 693- 701.

[31] Milaneschi Y, Corsi AM, Penninx BW, *et al.* Interleukin-1 receptor antagonist and incident depressive symptoms over 6 years in older persons: the InCHIANTI study. Biol Psychiatry 2009; 65: 973-978.

[32] Musselman DL, Lawson DH, Gumnick JF, *et al.* Paroxetine for the prevention of depression induced by high-dose interferon alfa. N Engl J Med 2001; 344: 961-966.

[33] Capuron L, Miller AH. Cytokines and psychopathology: lessons from interferon-alpha. Biol Psychiatry 2004; 56: 819-824.

[34] Raison CL, Demetrashvili M, Capuron L, Miller AH. Neuropsychiatric adverse effects of interferon-alpha: recognition and management. CNS Drugs 2005; 19: 105-123.

[35] Capuron L, Miller AH. Immune system to brain signaling: neuropsychopharmacological implications. Pharmacol Ther 2011; 130: 226-238.

[36] Cancello R, Henegar C, Viguerie N. Reduction of macrophage infiltration and chemoattractant gene expression changes in white adipose tissue of morbidly obese subjects after surgery-induced weight loss. Diabetes 2005; 54: 2277-2286.

[37] Caraci F, Copani A, Nicoletti F, Drago F. Depression and Alzheimer's disease: neurobiological links and common pharmacological targets. Eur J Pharmacol 2010; 626: 64-71.

[38] Maes M, Yirmyia R, Noraberg J, *et al.* The inflammatory & neurodegenerative (I&ND) hypothesis of depression: leads for future research and new drug developments in depression. Metab Brain Dis 2009; 24: 27-53.

[39] Krishnadas R, Cavanagh J. Depression: an inflammatory illness? J Neurol Neurosurg Psychiatry 2012; 83: 495-502.

[40] van Heesch F, Prins J, Korte-Bouws GA, *et al.* Systemic tumor necrosis factor-alpha decreases brain stimulation reward and increases metabolites of serotonin and dopamine in the nucleus accumbens of mice. Behav Brain Res 2013; 253: 191-195.

[41] Lucin KM, Wyss-Coray T. Immune activation in brain aging and neurodegeneration: too much or too little? Neuron 2009; 64: 110-122.

[42] Buga AM, Di Napoli M, Popa-Wagner A. Preclinical models of stroke in aged animals with or without comorbidities: role of neuroinflammation. Biogerontology 2013; 14: 651-662.

[43] Floyd RA. Antioxidants, oxidative stress, and degenerative neurological disorders. Proc Soc Exp Biol Med 1999; 222: 236-245.

[44] Ye SM, Johnson RW. Increased interleukin-6 expression by microglia from brain of aged mice. J Neuroimmunol 1999; 93: 139-148.

[45] Akiyama H, Barger S, Barnum S. Inflammation and Alzheimer's disease. Neurobiol Aging 2000; 21: 383-421.

[46] Streit WJ, Mrak RE, Griffin WS. Microglia and neuroinflammation: a pathological perspective. J Neuroinflamm 2004; 1: 14.

[47] Correll GE, Futter GE. Two case studies of patients with major depressive disorder given low-dose (subanesthetic) ketamine infusions. Pain Med 2006; 7: 92-95.

[48] Zarate CA Jr, Singh JB, Carlson PJ, *et al.* A randomized trial of an N-methyl-D-aspartate antagonist in treatment-resistant major depression. Arch Gen Psychiatry 2006; 63: 856-864.

[49] Li N, Lee B, Liu RJ, Banasr M, Dwyer JM, Iwata M, *et al.* mTOR-dependent synapse formation underlies the rapid antidepressant effects of NMDA antagonists. Science 2010; 329: 959-964.

[50] Duman RS, Li Nanxin, Liu Rong-Jian, *et al.* Signaling pathways underlying the rapid antidepressant actions of ketamine. Neuropharmacology 2012; 62: 35-41.

[51] Chandran A, Iyo AH, Jernigan CS, Legutko B, Austin MC,Karolewicz B. Reduced phosphorylation of the mTOR signaling pathway components in the amygdala of rats exposed to chronic stress. Prog Neuropsychopharmacol Biol Psychiatry 2013; 40: 240-245.

[52] Deschwanden A, Karolewicz B, Feyissa AM, *et al.* Reduced metabotropic glutamate receptor 5 density in major depression determined by [11C]ABP688 PET and postmortem study. Am J Psychiatry 2011.

[53] Feyissa AM, Woolverton WL, Miguel-Hidalgo JJ, *et al.* Elevated level of metabotropic glutamate receptor 2/3 in the prefrontal cortex in major depression. Prog Neuropsychopharmacol Biol Psychiatry 2010; 34: 279-283.

[54] Jernigan CS, Goswami DB, Austin MC,*et al.* The mTOR signaling pathway in the prefrontal cortex is compromised inmajor depressive disorder. Prog Neuropsychopharmacol Biol Psychiatry 2011; 35: 1774-1779.

[55] Santini E, Huynh TN, Klann E. Mechanisms of translation control underlying long-lasting synaptic plasticity and the consolidation of long-term memory. Prog Mol Biol Transl Sci 2014; 122: 131-167.

[56] Burke SN, Barnes CA. Neural plasticity in the ageing brain. Nat Rev Neurosci 2006; 7: 30-40.

[57] Buga AM, Margaritescu C, Scholz CJ, Radu E, Zelenak C, Popa-Wagner. Transcriptomics of post- stroke angiogenesis in the aged brain. Front Aging Neurosci 2013; 6: 44.

[58] Davalos D, Grutzendler J, Yang G, *et al.* ATP mediates rapid microglial response to local brain injury *in vivo*. Nat Neurosci 2005; 8: 752-758.

[59] Nimmerjahn A, Kirchhoff F, Helmchen F. Resting microglial cells are highly dynamic surveillants of brain parenchyma *in vivo*. Science 2005; 308: 1314-1318.

[60] Paolicelli RC, Bolasco G, Pagani F, *et al.* Synaptic pruning by microglia is necessary for normal brain development. Science 2011; 333: 1456-1458.

[61] Tremblay ME, Lowery RL, Majewska AK. Microglial interactions with synapses are modulated by visual experience. PLoS Biol 2010; 8: e1000527.

[62] Wake H, Moorhouse AJ, Jinno S, Kohsaka S, Nabekura J. Resting microglia directly monitor the functional state of synapses *in vivo* and determine the fate of ischemic terminals. J Neurosci 2009; 29: 3974-3980.

[63] Schafer DP, Lehrman EK, Stevens B. The ''quad-partite'' synapse: microglia-synapse interactions in the developing and mature CNS. Glia 2013; 61: 24-36.

[64] Hanisch UK, Kettenmann H. Microglia: active sensor and versatile effector cells in the normal and pathologic brain. Nat Neurosci 2007; 10: 1387-1394.

[65] Wakselman S, Be´chade C, Roumier A, *et al.* Developmental neuronal death in hippocampus requires the microglial CD11b integrin and DAP12 immunoreceptor. J Neurosci 2008; 28: 8138-8143.

[66] Krishnan KR, Taylor WD, McQuoid DR, *et al.* Clinical characteristics of magnetic resonance imaging-defined subcortical ischemic depression. Biol Psychiatry 2004; 55: 390-397.

[67] Downes CE, Crack PJ. Neural injury following stroke: are toll-like receptors the link between the immune system and the CNS? Br J Pharmacol 2010; 160: 1872-1888.

[68] Ransohoff RM, Cardona AE. The myeloid cells of the central nervous system parenchyma. Nature 2010; 468: 253-262.

[69] Becker KJ, Kalil AJ, Tanzi P, *et al.* Autoimmune responses to the brain after stroke are associated with worse outcome. Stroke 2011; 42: 2763-2769.

[70] Henry C, Huang Y, Wynne AM, Godbout JP. Peripheral lipopolysaccharide (LPS) challenge promotes microglial hyperactivity in aged mice that is associated with exaggerated induction of both proinflammatory IL-1 [beta] and anti-inflammatory IL-10 cytokines. Brain Behav Immun 2009; 23: 309-317.

[71] Palin K, Cunningham C, Forse P, Perry VH, Platt N. Systemic inflammation switches the inflammatory cytokine profile in CNS wallerian degeneration. Neurobiol Dis 2008; 30: 19-29

[72] Bilbo SD, Schwarz JM. Early-life programming of laterlife brain and behavior: a critical role for the immune system. Front Behav Neurosci 2009; 3: 14.

[73] Murray C, Sanderson DJ, Barkus C, *et al.* Systemic inflammation induces acute working memory deficits in the primed brain: relevance for delirium. Neurobiol Aging 2010; 33: 603-616.

[74] Godbout JP, Johnson RW. Age and neuroinflammation: a lifetime of psychoneuroimmune consequences. Neurol Clin 2006; 24: 521-538.

[75] DilgerRN, JohnsonRW. Aging, microglial cell priming, and the discordant central inflammatory response to signals from the peripheral immune system. J Leukoc Biol 2008; 84: 932-939.

[76] Surtees PG, Wainwright NW, Boekholdt SM, *et al.* Major depression, C-reactive protein, and incident ischemic heart disease in healthy men and women. Psychosom Med 2008; 70: 850-855.

[77] Maes M. Depression is an inflammatory disease, but cell mediated immune activation is the key component of depression. Prog Neuropsychopharmacol. Biol Psychiatry 2011; 35: 664-675.

[78] Taylor WD, Aizenstein HJ, Alexopoulos GS. The vascular depression hypothesis: mechanisms linking vascular disease with depression. Mol Psychiatry 2013; 18: 963-974

[79] Walker AK, Kavelaars A, Heijnen CJ, Dantzer R. Neuroinflammation and comorbidity of pain and depression. Pharmacol Rev 2013; 66: 80-101.

[80] Leonard BE. Inflammation, depression and dementia: are they connected? Neurochem Res 2007; 32: 1749-1756

[81] Rojo LE, Ferna´ndez JA, Maccioni AA, Jimenez JM, Maccioni RB. Neuroinflammation: implications for the pathogenesis and molecular diagnosis of Alzheimer's disease. Arch Med Res 2008; 39: 1-16.

[82] Byers AL, Vittinghoff E, Lui LY, *et al.* Twenty-year depressive trajectories among older women. Arch Gen Psychiatry 2012; 69: 1073-1079.

[83] Paranthaman R, Greenstein AS, Burns AS, *et al.* Vascular function in older adults with depressive disorder. Biol Psychiatry 2010; 68: 133-139.

[84] Greenstein AS, Paranthaman R, Burns A, *et al.* Cerebrovascular damage in late-life depression is associated with structural and functional abnormalities of subcutaneous small arteries. Hypertension 2010; 56: 734-740.

[85] Broadley AJ, Korszun A, Jones CJ, Frenneaux MP. Arterial endothelial function is impaired in treated depression. Heart 2002; 88: 521-523.

[86] Moody DM, Bell MA, Challa VR. Features of the cerebral vascular pattern that predict vulnerability to perfusion or oxygenation deficiency: an anatomic study. Am J Neuroradiol 1990; 11: 431-439.

[87] Matsushita K, Kuriyama Y, Nagatsuka K, *et al.* Periventricular white matter lucency and cerebral blood flow autoregulation in hypertensive patients. Hypertension 1994; 23: 565-568.

[88] Berg A, Psych L, Lönnqvist J, Palomäki H, Kaste M. Assessment of Depression After Stroke.A Comparison of Different Screening Instruments. Stroke 2009; 40: 523-529.

[89] Quaranta D, Marra C, Gainotti G. Mood disorders after stroke: diagnostic validation of the poststroke depression rating scale. Cerebrovasc Dis 2008; 23: 237-43.

[90] Figiel, GS, Epstein C, McDonald WM, *et al.* The use of rapid-rate transcranial magnetic stimulation (rTMS) in refractory depressed patients. JNeuropsychiatry Clin Neurosci 1998; 10: 20-25.

[91] Klein E, Kreinin I, Chistyakov A. Therapeutic efficacy of right prefrontal slow repetitive transcranial magnetic stimulation in major depression. Arch Gen Psychiatry 1999; 56: 315-320.

[92] Manes F, Jorge R, Morcuende M, Yamada T, Paradiso S, Robinson RG. A controlled study of repetitive transcranial magnetic stimulation as a treatment of depression in the elderly. Int Psychogeriatr 2001; 13: 225-231.

[93] Mosimann UP, Schmitt W, Greenberg BD, *et al.* Repetitive transcranial magnetic stimulation: a putative add-on treatment for major depression in elderly patients. Psychiatry Res 2004; 126: 123- 133.

[94] Fregni F, Marcolin MA, Myczkowski M, *et al.* Predictors of antidepressant response in clinical trials of transcranial magnetic stimulation. Int J Neuropsychopharmacol 2005; 9: 1-14.

[95] Milev R, Abraham G, Hasey G, Cabaj JL. Repetitive transcranial magnetic stimulation for treatment of medication-resistant depression in older adults. J ECT 2009; 25: 24-49

[96] Nahas Z, Li X, Kozel FA, *et al.* Safety and benefits of distance-adjusted prefrontal transcranial magnetic stimulation in depressed patients 55-75 years of age: a pilot study. Depress Anxiety 2004; 19: 249-256.

[97] Raison CL, Rutherford RE, Woolwine BJ, *et al.* A randomized controlled trial of the tumor necrosis factor antagonist infliximab for treatment-resistant depression: the role of baseline inflammatory biomarkers. JAMA Psychiatry 2013; 70: 31-41.

[98] Di Napoli M, Shah IM. Neuroinflammation and cerebrovascular disease in old age: a translational medicine perspective. J Aging Res 2011; 857484.

Chapter 4: Molecular Insights into Depression in the Genomic Era

CHAPTER 4

Molecular Insights into Depression in the Genomic Era

Manjit Singh and Changanamkandath Rajesh*

Department of Biotechnology, Sri Guru Granth Sahib World University, Fatehgarh Sahib, Punjab, India

Abstract: Several psychiatric disorders including Schizophrenia, major depressive disorder (MDD), bipolar disorder, attention-deficit/hyperactivity disorder and autism spectrum disorder are all very common. WHO data suggest MDD as a leading cause of adult disability, however the complex nature of the disease etiology makes it least understood among its more studied disease counterparts. Although both genetic and environmental factors are known to contribute substantially to the etiology of MDD, several association studies both single gene and Genome Wide Association Studies (GWAS) are available describing the contribution of multiple genes. Severe lacunae exist in correlation among these association studies that prevent a clear definition in genetic causes that could be a result of small samples, epigenesis, heterozygosity in populations studied, presence of rare variations as well as lack of proper co-relation with environmental factors. With the advances in nucleic acid and amino acid sequencing techniques in this era of genomics and proteomics, the identification of novel disease markers is easier. More extensive study identifying rare variations in larger population along with a more systematic study including system pathways as well as genetic and protein interaction is recommended to obtain a clear picture of the underlying genetic causes of these complex disorders.

Keywords: Biomarkers, Candidate genes, Depression, Epigenetics, Genome Wide Association Studies (GWAS), Genomics, Major depressive disorder (MDD), Pharmacogenetics, psychiatric disorders, Serotonin transporter (5HTT).

INTRODUCTION

Clinical depression or Major Depressive Disorder (MDD) is a part of several complex psychiatric disorders that include Schizophrenia, bipolar disorder, attention-deficit/hyperactivity disorder and autism spectrum disorder (Table **1**). These psychiatric disorders are pretty common in world population [1], with a very high rate of morbidity and mortality [2, 3].

***Corresponding author Changanamkandath Rajesh:** Department of Biotechnology, Sri Guru Granth Sahib World University, Fatehgarh Sahib-140406, Punjab, India; E-mails: rajeshc@sggswu.org; rajhs2000@yahoo.com

Puneetpal Singh and Sarabjit Mastana (Eds)

Table 1. Summary of major psychiatric disorders (Doherty and Owen, 2014).

Disease	Symptoms	Age of Onset	Prescription
Attention - deficit/Hyperactivity disorder (ADHD)	Inattention, Hyperactivity, Impulsivity	7-12 years	Psycho stimulants as methylphenidate
Autism Spectrum Disorder (ASD)	Deficits in social communication, social interaction, Restricted, repetitive behaviors, Hallucinations, Delusions	<3 years	None recommended
Schizophrenia	Hallucinations, Delusions, Disorganized speech or behavior Apathy, Lack of emotional reactivity	16-30	Antipsychotics as risperidone
Bipolar disorder	Discrete episodes of elevated, irritable or agitated mood, Episodes of low mood Hallucinations, Delusions	18-40	Mood stabilizers as Lithium and antipsychotics as olanzapine
Major Depressive Disorder	Low mood, Loss of interest or pleasure, Lack of energy, Psychosis	20-45	Antidepressants as citalopram

Phenotypes of depression are also classified based on severe symptoms of Bipolar I disorder (BPI), or mania and depression, less severe disease phenotype of bipolar II disorder (BPII) or hypomania and depression, and BPIII, includes recurrent depressive syndromes [4]. MDD is characterized by several symptoms including low mood, low self-esteem, inappropriate guilt, thoughts of death and suicide, diminished concentration, loss of interest or pleasure in normally enjoyable activities and disturbance of sleep and appetite. Data from United States show that around 3% of MDD patients commit suicide, but more importantly about 60% of people committing suicide have been diagnosed with MDD [5]. The mortality is also associated with an increased risk of allied ailments throughout the body as a result of MDD including atherosclerosis, heart disease, hypertension, stroke, cognitive decline and dementia (including Alzheimer's disease), osteoporosis, immune impairments, obesity, metabolic syndrome, insulin resistance and type 2 diabetes [6]. Most of these psychiatric disorders including MDD are multifactorial diseases arising from a combination of genetic predisposition in conjunction with environmental factors. This has prevented the advent of any significant biomarkers that have been associated with these disorders in spite of large amount of studies reported on these [7-11].

The current diagnostic classifications for these disorders are descriptive based on several co-occurring symptoms. This diagnostic inefficiency results in delay in treatment and low patient compliance. Due to the multi-drug approach currently employed, patient response is also unpredictable and usually unfavourable. The variability in dosages prescribed also hinders satisfactory response as well as development of adverse side effects. Although the response to drugs is attributed to multiple physiological and environmental factors including age, kidney and liver metabolism, dietary and personal habits, genetic co-relation to drug effect has never been doubted [12]. With the advances in the field of pharmacogenetics and pharmogenomics it is about time that the age-old method of trial and error in treatment strategies be replaced with personalized treatment using effective drugs that would show better response to the right kind of medication.

Although, levels of multiple biochemical markers including glucocorticoids, neurosteroids, glucose and insulin levels, pro- and anti-inflammatory cytokines and oxidative stress markers have been shown to vary in depression, these do not serve as definite markers for diagnosis [6]. Advances in Genomics have led to new hope in identification of novel genetic markers emerging as identifiers of underlying causes of these diseases as well as for effective treatment responses. This chapter attempts to compile the data available in these studies and look at genetic studies in the field of psychiatry especially focusing on MDD.

GENETIC DISEASE MARKER

A variety of biomarkers can be identified for diagnosis and course of the disease (Type 0 biomarkers), effect of drug intervention (Type 1 biomarkers) and surrogate end points of a clinical course (Type 2 biomarkers) [13]. The methods used to diagnose depression included behavioral approaches, brain mapping techniques or electrophysiological techniques. Early genetic biomarker identification strategies of segregation analysis and transmission patterns in genetic models, analysis of genetic vulnerability traits and linkage studies with classical genetic markers did yield significant results [4]. Polymorphic DNA markers also provided early success in psychiatric genetics but subsequent linkage evidence was not significant enough [14, 15].

Multiple linkage studies have reported suggestive evidence for association of depression to multiple chromosomal regions. These include *Chromosome1q31-32*, *Chromosome 10p14*, *Chromosome 13q31-32* and *Chromosome 18p11*region associated with Depression and Schizophrenia [16, 17], *Chromosome 4p16*, associated with mental health wellness [18], *Chromosome 6pter-p24* [19],

Chromosome 12q23-24 [20] and *Chromosome 18q21-23* [21] associated with multiple psychiatric disorders. However, there has not been enough evidence of association of any of these chromosomal regions to specific candidate genes associated with depression other than a few as Golf, a G-protein receptor gene in region of *Chromosome 18p11*. This contradiction in results of association of identified genes or genetic loci to clinical symptoms in multiple studies has not yet helped clinicians in providing clear diagnosis based on these genetic markers.

CANDIDATE GENE STUDIES IN DEPRESSION

Candidate genes for depression are the genes with presumed functional relevance for the depression phenotype. Studies have identified multiple candidate genes where SNPs and mutations have been reported that have effect on depression phenotypes (Table **2**). The different candidate genes and associated study however has not been definite with contrasting data reporting significance and few others not demonstrating significant association to MDD. One of the major classes of candidate genes are the genes involved in monoamine synthesis and transport and associated G proteins [22]. This includes monoamine oxidase type A (*MAOA*) that is involved in degradation of biological amines as dopamine, noradrenaline, 5-hydroxytryptamine (5-HT). Few alleles and homozygous genotype association of the high-activity variants, particularly in females [23-25] and low-activity alleles with MDD and depressive symptoms are reported [26]. Certain other potential candidate genes that are responsible in regulation of monoamines include Corticotropin Releasing Hormone (*CRH*) and Brain Derived Neurotrophic Factor (*BDNF*) [27, 28].

Serotonin transporter (*5HTT*) and serotonin receptor genes (*HTR*) are second class of genes that have been studied as candidate genes. A functional 44-base-pair (bp) indel polymorphism, in the regulatory region of the human *5HTT* gene named as the serotonin-transporter-linked polymorphic region, *5HTTLPR* [28], regulates with differential transcriptional expression activity of *5HTT* as well as 5-HT reuptake in lymphoblastoid cell lines [29]. The second reported significant association study involves the 16/17-bp VNTR in second intron of the transporter *5HTT* gene. There is suggestive evidence of association of functional polymorphism, G816C (rs6296), in Serotonin receptor gene 1A, *HTR1A*, and a more severe recurrent form of depression [30]. No strong association has emerged with other receptor genes including *HTR12A, HTR3A, HTR3B, HTR5A* and *HTR6,* except few suggestive data [31]. *HTR2C,* is located on the *Chromosome Xq24*, has a functional polymorphism C23S (rs6318) which is interesting for further investigation due to the sexual bias that has been observed in depression.

Table 2. Few candidate genes with a role in MDD phenotype.

S. No.	Marker	Role in Depression	References
1.	Corticotropin Releasing Hormone (*CRH*)	responsible for regulation of monoamines	Wuwongse *et al.*, 2010
2.	Brain Derived Neurotrophic Factor (*BDNF*)	Neurotrophin responsible for regulation of monoamine found in the brain.	Wuwongse *et al.*, 2010,
3.	Monoamine Oxidase A (*MAO-A*),	Mutations resulted in psychiatric disturbances, including depressive behaviors	Haavik *et al.*, 2008
4.	Catechol-Methyltransferase	Mutations resulted in psychiatric disturbances, including depressive behaviors	Jaabi *et al.*, 2008
5.	Serotonin Transporter (*5-HTT*)	Mutations resulted in psychiatric disturbances, including depressive behaviors	Heils *et al.*, 1996; Huang *et al.*, 2003
6.	Indoleamine-pyrrole 2,3-Dioxygenase (*IDO*)	Involved in cytokine- induced depression by reduced serotonin synthesis and reduction in tryptophan level accompanied by increased levels of neurotoxic kynurenine.	Wichers *et al.*, 2005
7.	Cytokine IL-1b	Involved in depression and Alzeimer's. A polymorphism in the promoter region of IL-1b results in at high risk of developing depression.	McCulley *et al.*, 2004
8.	Tryptophan Hydroxylase (*TPH1*)	A key enzyme in 5HT synthesis. *TPH1* polymorphisms have been associated with depression phenotypes.	Tan *et al.*, 2003; Viikki *et al.*, 2010; Gizatullin *et al.*, 2006
9.	Tyrosine Hydroxylase (*TH*)	A key enzyme in dopamine synthesis. TH inhibition may cause depressive symptoms in healthy subjects.	Opmeer *et al.*, 2010
10.	*CREB1*	CREB1 transcription factor regulates the expression of growth factors involved in synaptogenesis and neurogenesis.	Duman *et al.*, 1999
11.	*SLC6A4*	Encodes the protein that is a therapeutic target of selective serotonin reuptake inhibition drugs.	Lesch *et al.*, 1996
12.	Piccolo (*PCLO*) gene	Important in serotonergic neurotransmission.	Hek *et al.*, 2010
13.	Bicaudal C homologue 1 (*BICC1*)	An RNA binding protein that forms complex interactions with RNA and other proteins associated with neuropsychiatric diseases.	Lewis *et al.*, 2010
14.	*CACNA1C*	L-typeVoltage gated calcium channel subunit involved in calcium channel signalling.	Ferreira *et al.*, 2008
15.	methyl CpG binding protein 2 gene (*MECP2*)	Mutations in the *MECP2* have been shown to lead to neurodevelopmental deficits, such as those associated with Rett syndrome.	Samaco and Neul 2011
16.	*ZBTB20*	Epigenesis in *ZBTB20* is significantly associated with Depression. *ZBTB20* plays critical role in regionalization and volume of the archicortex, which plays a role in depression.	Davies *et al.*, 2014

A couple of polymorphisms within Tryptophan hydroxylase gene, *TPH1,* involved in the biosynthesis of 5HT have been suggested for association with depression like A218C polymorphism (rs1800532) and an intronic C779A (rs1799913) [32, 33]. Although a loss of function substitution, R144H, in a second isoform of the gene, *TPH2*, has been observed, the occurrence of the variant is relatively rare [34]. Multiple polymorphisms in the Noradrenaline transporter gene, *SLC6A2*, and in adrenaline and noradrenaline receptors, *ADRA2A* and *ADRB1,* Dopamine receptor genes, *DRD1, DRD2* and *DRD3* and Dopamine transporter gene, *DAT1* all in the monoamine pathway have been suggestively implicated in depression.

Additional genes over the monoamine pathway, that have been associated with depression include Brain-Derived Neurotrophic Factor (*BDNF*), *GOLF*, G-protein coupled receptor, dopamine D5 receptor (*DRD5*), a GABA receptor (*GABRB1*), and Wolfram syndrome (*WFS1*), Piccolo (*PCLO*) gene, Bicaudal C homologue 1 (*BICC1*) *etc*. (Table **2**).

The list of genes in this category are long, however, there are contrasting evidence of direct association of these candidate genes with depression like other complex disorders including Cardiovascular or diabetes, psychiatric disorders also do not follow a mendelian pattern of inheritance. More exhaustive studies need to be done covering a more exhaustive sample collection and taking the environmental conditions and other variable factors into consideration.

Genome Wide Association Studies (GWAS) due to recent advances as Array-based strategies and Next-Generation sequencing technologies can be used to perform such high throughput studies and such studies have now been undertaken on a large scale. Such GWAS studies are starting to reveal newer SNPs associations and additional pathways than the ones already known that can be more promising. One such GWAS study identifies four SNPs associated with five different psychiatric disorders [35]. Two of these reported in *CACNA1C* and *CACNB2* genes, are part of L-type Voltage-gated calcium-channel subunits, indicating the involvement of calcium channels in psychiatric disorders. *CACNA1C* polymorphism has been previously reported in other GWAS studies as well, to be associated with Schizophrenia, bipolar disorders and MDD [36]. Multiple GWAS studies show several common SNPs associated with multiple psychiatric disorders. Few polymorphisms in candidate genes for MDD identified by such studies are *PCLO* (piccolo presynaptic cytomatrix protein) implicated with monoaminergenic transmission [37], novel locus, BICC1 [38], *ATP6V1B2*,

SP4 and *GRM7* [39, 40]. Such GWAS studies will also provide additional conclusive evidences to suggestive candidate genes that are already under study. Meta and mega analysis is currently underway as part of psychiatric consortium to find correlation between SNPs associated with MDD patients.

COPY NUMBER VARIATIONS IN DEPRESSION

Lack of strong correlation of common SNPs to depression from multiple GWAS studies has compelled the researchers to examine other types of genetic variations in such disorders. Copy number variations are a significant class of such genetic variations, which form a rare structural class of variants present in <1% population. Rare copy number variations have been identified in multiple psychiatric disorders described earlier including Schizophrenia, mood disorders, and bipolar disorders [41-43]. In a recent GWAS study, >100 kbp deletion enrichment is observed in MDD patients that needs to be investigated for further research [44]. Although this is one of the few studies, which associates copy number variations directly to clinical depression phenotype, Micro deletions and duplications in several genes associated with synaptic signaling, neuronal migration, neurotransmitter metabolism and myelination are reported in Schizophrenia [45]. The copy number of variations has also been associated with decreased occurrence of Schizophrenia [46].

EPIGENETICS IN DEPRESSION

Epigenetics is fast emerging as an important investigation mechanism to understand gene expression in a variety of complex disorders and MDD has also been investigated in this category. This developing field can serve to predict future susceptibility diagnostic markers for MDD as well as help develop newer therapeutic strategies [47]. Epigenesis refers to any DNA sequence independent regulation of gene expression and mainly covers DNA promoter methylation as well as histone methylation and acetylation. Recently another epigenetic modulator that has emerged as a key player in several diseases are microRNAs or miRNAs. The stress and depression encountered in early life could therefore result in persistent expression differences of multiple genes.

Epigenetic modulation of a range of genes has been reported using studies of early stress given to mice. This includes the genes coding for Brain derived neurotrophic factor (*BDNF*), Corticotrophin Releasing Hormone (*CRH*), DNA methyltransferase protein, Glutamate decarboxylase (*GAD67*) and reelin [47]. The methylation pattern of candidate genes of depression including *BNDG*, glucocorticoid receptor and serotonin receptors are seen in children exposed to prenatal stress [48, 50]. Recent data on mice models and human samples indicate a range of pre- and post-natal stress factors that can lead to long-term or permanent epigenetic regulation of depression-related genes.

Human data using a Genome wide methylation pattern as well as individual candidate genes of depression indicate a range of DNA methylation and chromatin activation status. *BDNF* gene and its receptor Trk B has been of special interest due to decreased mRNA levels of these proteins having a co-relation to methylation of the CpG islands [51]. Similar methylation of the CpG sites and Histone 3 at lysine 27 has been observed in *Trk B-T1,* a truncated form of BDNF receptor [52, 53].

miRNA directed regulation of depression genes has also been reported in multiple studies. A global study of miRNA levels in depressed suicide cohort demonstrate a down regulation in genes implicated in depression as vascular endothelial growth factor and B-cell- CLL/lymphoma 2, and in the epigenetic control of gene expression including DNA methyltransferase 3b [54]. Epigenetic studies on candidate gene expression and miRNAs are also being performed to understand the mechanism of action of drugs used to treat depression. This emerging field could serve in future as a target for diagnostic and therapeutic development.

PHARMACOGENETICS AND PHARMACOGENOMICS OF DEPRESSION

The emergence of the field of pharmacogenetics and personalized medicine has now been revolutionizing the field of medicine such that the one-drug-for-all therapy may not any longer be the way forward. The molecular studies and development from the studies of depression will have their maximum effect on this field of pharmacogenetics providing patients with a greater chance of positive antidepressant response. Although the aim of such personalized therapy is still not available, there are several potential polymorphisms in several candidate genes of depression that have been shown to have a role in antidepressant treatment [55].

One of the most convincing evidence of pharmacogenetics and pharmacokinetics emerges from the metabolizing capacity of various genetic polymorphisms in the Cytochrome P450 variants [56]. Knowledge of the metabolizing capacity of the patient will be important before prescription of any antidepressant and its dose in order to avoid serious side effects. Few specific examples of role of polymorphisms on antidepressant drug uptake involve those targeting serotonin transporters [57]. Multiple variants of the serotonin transporter gene have been investigated for drug response and there are quite a few examples of differential response to definite phenotypes. A well studied example with maximum association with antidepressant response in Asian samples is a 17 bp variable number tandem repeats.

Three other genes within which variation is responsible for drug response include serotonin receptor 1A, serotonin receptor 2A and tryptophan hydroxylase A C1019G (rs6295) polymorphism in the upstream regulatory region of Serotonin receptor 1A, HTR1A, is associated with weak interaction of Deafl and Hes5 repressors [58]. There are similar multiple variations in the receptor 2A and Tryptophan hydroxylase gene that has been investigated extensively for effect of antidepressants. In addition, G protein beta 3 subunit polymorphism [59], FK506 binding protein 5 gene, *FKBP5* [60], corticotrophin releasing hormone receptor gene, *CRH* [61] are all candidate genes that have been investigated for their role in variety of drug responses. Proteomic studies have also been used to understand the role of the drugs in biomarker studies especially in response to drug treatment [62].

CONCLUSION

It is relatively clear that MDD and other psychiatric disorders are complex disorders with multiple metabolic, genetic and environmental factors affecting the disease etiology. The genetic factors, though extremely important, have failed to generate the impact that is expected from such association mainly due to a lack of consistent results from the population studies. This could be a result of genetic and phenotypic heterogeneity, low sample sizes used, lack of proper controls *etc*.

There are several genetic factors that are associated with multiple psychiatric disorders with a very clear overlap of the genetic architecture among these disorders. Like clinical and epidemiological evidences, the genetic factors responsible for one psychiatric disorder are also associated with several other disorders. Chromosomal locus *22q11.2* that is a reported strongest risk factor for Schizophrenia is also associated with other neuronal disorders as Autism Spectrum Disorder (ASD), Attention-Defecit/Hyperactivity Disorder (ADHD), mood disorders and Anxiety disorders [63]. However, this complexity in association of genetic factors is no different from the various behavioral, neuroimaging and clinical phenotypes currently used in diagnosis. Therefore, the improvement of current diagnostic systems is necessary to include genetic markers as well.

In this modern era of genomics and proteomics, it is clear that multi-targeted studies can be performed and the sample limitations do not arise to understand the complex networks of genetic architecture in MDD and related disorders. Also, the sequencing of human genome has given us a large amount of important data on the presence of variants and a new hope of being able to unravel the genetic pre-disposition of several diseases. In addition it will help design effective personalized treatment regimens that are tailored for each individual and minimizes side effects. Exploiting these genomic tools along with proteomic analysis of the samples can reveal new markers as well as validate already existing markers in psychiatric disorders.

In spite of all these advances, the complexity of the disease and lack of clear definition for each of the psychiatric disorder will still be a definite challenge in delineating the precise role of each polymorphism. However, use of sufficiently large sample sizes taking into consideration all environmental and other factors, it will be possible to unearth associations that will be useful in precise diagnosis and treatment.

CONFLICT OF INTERESTS

The authors have no conflict of interests to declare.

ACKNOWLEDGEMENTS

Declared None.

REFERENCES

[1] Kessler RC, Angermeyer M, Anthony JC, *et al.* Lifetime prevalence and age-of-onset distributions of mental disorders in the world health organization's world mental health survey initiative. World Psychiatry 2007; 6:168-176.

[2] Murray CJ, Lopez AD. Global mortality, disability, and the contribution of risk factors: Global Burden of Disease Study. Lancet 1997; 349: 1436-1442.

[3] Whiteford HA, Degenhardt L, Rehm J, *et al.* Global burden of disease attributable to mental and substance use disorders: findings from the Global Burden of Disease Study 2010. Lancet 2013; 382: 1575-1586.

[4] Baron M. Manic-depression genes and the new millennium: poised for discovery. Mol Psychiatry 2002; 7: 342-358.

[5] DiMatteo MR, Lepper HS, Croghan TW. Depression is a risk factor for noncompliance with medical treatment: metaanalysis of the effects of anxiety and depression on patient adherence. Arch Intern Med 2000; 160: 2101-2107.

[6] Wolkowitz, OM, Reus VI, Mellon SH. Of sound mind and body: depression, disease, and accelerated aging. Dialogues Clin Neurosci 2011; 13: 25-39.

[7] Taylor L, Faraone SV, Tsuang MT. Family, twin and adoption studies of bipolar disease. Curr Psychiatry Rep 2002; 4: 130-133.

[8] Shih RA, Belmonte PL, Zandi PP. A review of the evidence from family, twin and adoption studies for a genetic contribution to adult psychiatric disorders. Int Rev Psychiatry 2004; 16: 260-283.

[9] Thapar A, Cooper M, Jefferies R, Stergiakouli E. What causes attention deficit hyperactivity disorder? Arch Dis Child 2012; 97: 260-265.

[10] Szatmari P, Jones MB, Zwaigenbaum L, MacLean JE. Genetics of autism: overview and new directions. J Autism Dev Disord 1998; 28: 351-368.

[11] Wray NR, Gottesman II. Using summary data from the Danish national registers to estimate heritabilities for schizophrenia, bipolar disorder, and major depressive disorder. Front Genet, 2012; 3: 118

[12] Bondy B. Pharmacogenomics in depression and antidepressants. Dialogues Clin Neurosci 2005; 7: 223-230

[13] Lesko LJ, Atkinson AJ Jr. Use of biomarkers and surrogate endpoints in drug development and regulatory decisionmaking: criteria, validation, strategies. Annu Rev Pharmacol Toxicol. 2001; 41: 347-366.

[14] Martin JB. Molecular genetics: applications to the clinical neurosciences. Science 1987; 238: 765-772.

[15] Kelsoe JR, Ginns EI, Egeland JA, *et al.* Re-evaluation of the linkage relationship between chromosome11p loci and the gene for bipolar affective disorder in the Old Order Amish. Nature 1989; 342: 238-243.

[16] Detera-Wadleigh SD, Badner JA, Berrettini WH, *et al.* A high-density genome scan detects evidence for a bipolar disorder susceptibility locus on 13q32 and other potential loci on 1q32 and 18p11.2. Proc Natl Acad Sci USA 1999; 96: 5604-5609.

[17] Vorstman JA, Anney RJ, Derks EM, *et al.* Autism Genome Project, the International Schizophrenia Consortium: No evidence that common genetic risk variation is shared between schizophrenia and autism. Am J Med Genet B Neuropsychiatr Genet 2013; 162B: 55-60.

[18] de la Serna E, Baeza I, Toro J, *et al.* Relationship between clinical and neuropsychological characteristics in child and adolescent first degree relatives of subjects with schizophrenia. Schizophr Res, 2010; 116: 159-167.

[19] Ferreira MA, O'Donovan MC, Meng YA, *et al.* Collaborative genomewide association analysis supports a role for ANK3 and CACNA1C in bipolar disorder. Nat Genet 2008; 40: 1056-1058.

[20] O'Donovan MC, Craddock N, Norton N, *et al.* Identification of loci associated with schizophrenia by genome-wide association and followup. Nat Genet 2008; 40: 1053-1055.

[21] McIntosh AM, Gow A, Luciano M, *et al.* Polygenic risk for schizophrenia is associated with cognitive change between childhood and old age. Biol Psychiatry 2013; 73: 938-943.

[22] Woods SC, Craig IW and McGuffin, P. The current state of play on the molecular genetics of depression. Psychol Med 2013; 43: 673-687.

[23] Schulze TG, Muller DJ, Krauss H, *et al.* Association between a functional polymorphism in the monoamine oxidase A gene promoter and major depressive disorder. American Journal of Medical Gen 2000; 96: 801-803.

[24] Yu YW, Chen TJ, Wang YC, *et al.* Association analysis for neuronal nitric oxide synthase gene polymorphism with major depression and fluoxetine response. Neuropsychobiology 2003; 47: 137-140.

[25] Rivera M, Gutierrez B, Molina E, *et al.* High-activity variants of the uMAOA polymorphism increase the risk for depression in a large primary care sample. Am J Med Genet. Part B, Neuropsychiatr Genet 2009; 150B: 395-402.

[26] Brummett BH, Krystal AD, Siegler IC, *et al.* Associations of a regulatory polymorphism of monoamine oxidase-A gene promoter (MAOA-uVNTR) with symptoms of depression and sleep quality. Psychosom Med 2007; 69: 396-401.

[27] Wuwongse S, Raymond Chuen-Chung Chang, Andrew CK. Law. The putative neurodegenerative links between depression and Alzheimer's Disease. Prog Neurobiol 2010; 91: 362-375.

[28] Heils A, Teufel A, Petri S, *et al.* Allelic variation of human serotonin transporter gene expression. J Neurochem 1996; 66: 2621-2624.

[29] Lesch KP, Bengel D, Heils A, *et al.* Association of anxiety-related traits with a polymorphism in the serotonin transporter gene regulatory region. Science 1996; 274: 1527-1531.

[30] Huang E J, Reichardt LF. Neurotrophins: roles in neuronal development and function. Ann Rev Neurosci 2001; 24: 677-736.

[31] Yamada K, Hattori E, Iwayama Y, *et al.* Distinguishable haplotype blocks in the HTR3A and HTR3B region in the Japanese reveal evidence of association of HTR3B with female major depression. Biological Psychiatry 2006; 60: 192-201.

[32] Tan EC, Chan AO, Tan CH, *et al.* Case-control and linkage disequilibrium studies of the tryptophan hydroxylase gene polymorphisms and major depressive disorder. Psychiatric Genetics 2003; 13: 151-154.

[33] Viikki M, Kampman O, Illi A, *et al.* TPH1 218A/C polymorphism is associated with major depressive disorder and its treatment response. Neurosci Lett 2010; 468: 80-84.

[34] Zhang X, Gainetdinov RR, Beaulieu JM, *et al.* Loss-of-function mutation in tryptophan hydroxylase-2 identified in unipolar major depression. Neuron 2005; 45: 11-16

[35] Cross-Disorder Group of the Psychiatric Genomics Consortium: Identification of risk loci with shared effects on five major psychiatric disorders: a genome-wide analysis. Lancet 2013; 381: 1371-1379.

[36] Ferreira MA, O'Donovan MC, Meng YA, *et al.* Collaborative genomewide association analysis supports a role for ANK3 and CACNA1C in bipolar disorder. Nat Genet 2008; 40: 1056-1058.

[37] Sullivan PF, de Geus EJ, Willemsen G, *et al.* Genome-wide association for major depressive disorder: a possible role for the presynaptic protein piccolo. Mol Psychiatry 2009; 14: 359-375.

[38] Lewis CM, Ng MY, Butler AW, *et al.* Genome-wide association study of major recurrent depression in the U.K. population. Am J Psychiatry 2010; 167: 949-957.

[39] Muglia P, Tozzi F, Galwey NW, *et al.* Genome-wide association study of recurrent major depressive disorder in two European case-control cohorts. Mol Psychiatry 2009; 15: 589-601.

[40] Shi J, Potash JB, Knowles JA, *et al.* Genome-wide association study of recurrent early-onset major depressive disorder. Mol Psychiatry 2011; 16: 193-201.

[41] Walsh T, McClellan JM, McCarthy SE, *et al.* Rare structural variants disrupt multiple genes in neurodevelopmental pathways in schizophrenia. Science 2008; 320: 539-543.

[42] Grozeva D, Kirov G, Conrad DF, *et al.* Reduced burden of very large and rare CNVs in bipolar affective disorder. Bipolar Disord, 2013; 15: 893-898.

[43] Malhotra D, McCarthy S, Michaelson JJ, *et al.* High frequencies of *de novo* CNVs in bipolar disorder and schizophrenia. Neuron 2011; 72: 951-963.

[44] Rucker JJ, Breen G, Pinto D, *et al.* Genome-wide association analysis of copy number variation in recurrent depressive disorder. Mol Psychiatry 2013; 18: 183-189.

[45] Stefansson H, Meyer-Lindenberg A, Steinberg S, *et al.* CNVs conferring risk of autism or schizophrenia affect cognition in controls. Nature 2014; 505: 361-366.

[46] Rees E, Kirov G, Sanders A, *et al.* Evidence that duplications of 22q11.2 protect against schizophrenia. Mol Psychiatry 2014; 19: 37-40.

[47] Dalton VS, Kolshus E and McLoughlin, DM. Epigenetics and depression: return of the repressed. J Affect Disord 2014; 155: 1-12.

[48] Toledo-Rodriguez,M,Lotfipour, S, Leonard G, Perron M, *et al.* Maternal smoking during pregnancy is associated with epigenetic modifications of the brain-derived neurotrophic factor-6 exon in adolescent offspring. Am J Med Genet B Neuropsychiatr Genet 2010; 153B: 1350-1354.

[49] Devlin AM, Brain U, Austin J, Oberlander TF. Prenatal exposure to maternal depressed mood and the MTHFR C677T variant affect SLC6A4 methylation in infants at birth. PLoS One 2010; 5: e12201.

[50] Radtke KM,Ruf M, Gunter HM, Dohrmann K, *et al.*Transgenerational impact of intimate partner violence on methylation in the promoter of the glucocorticoid receptor.Transl Psychiatry 2011; 1: e21.

[51] Keller S, Sarchiapone M, Zarrllii F, Videtic A, *et al.* Increased BDNF promoter methylation in the Wernicke area of suicide subjects. Arch Gen Psychiatry 2010; 67: 258-267.

[52] Ernst C, Chen ES, Turecki G. Histonemethylation and decreased expression of TrkB.T1in orbital frontal cortex of suicide completers. Mol Psychiatry 2009; 14: 830-832.

[53] Ernst C. Deleva V, Deng X, Sequeira A, *et al.* Alternative splicing, methylationstate, and expression profile of tropomyosin-related kinaseB in the frontal cortex of suicide completers. Arch Gen Psychiatry 2009; 66: 22-32.

[54] Smalheiser NR, Lugli G, Rizavi HS, *et al.* MicroRNA expression is down-regulated and reorganized in prefrontal cortex of depressed suicide subjects. PLoS One 2012; 7: e33201

[55] Drago A, De-Ronchi D and Serretti A. Pharmacogenetics of antidepressant response: An update. Human genomics 2009; 3: 257-274.

[56] Maier W, Zobel A. Contribution of allelic variations to the phenotype of response to antidepressants and antipsychotics. Eur Arch Psychiatry Clin Neurosci 2008; 258: 12-20.

[57] Meyer JH, Kapur S, Eisfeld B, *et al.*The effect of paroxetine on 5-HT(2A) receptors in depression: An [(18)F]setoperone PET imaging study, Am J Psychiatry 2001; 158: 78-85.

[58] Lemonde S, Turecki G, Bakish, D, *et al.* Impaired transrepression at a 5-hydroxytryptamine 1A receptor gene polymorphism associated with major depression and suicide, J Neurosci 2003; 23: 8788-8799.

[59] Siffert W, Rosskopf D, Siffert G, *et al.* Association of a human G-protein beta3 subunit variant with hypertension. Nat Genet 1998; 18: 45-48.

[60] Binder E, Salyakina D, Lichtner P, *et al.* Polymorphisms in FKBP5 are associated with increased recurrence of depressive episodes and rapid response to antidepressant treatment. Nat Genet 2004; 36: 1319-1325.

[61] Liu Z, Zhu F, Wang G, *et al.* Association study of corticotropin-releasing hormone receptor gene polymorphisms and antidepressant response in major depressive disorders. Neurosci Lett 2007; 414: 155-158.

[62] Martins-de-Souza D, Harris LW, Guest PC, Turck CW, Bahn S. The role of proteomics in depression research. Eur Arch Psychiatry Clin Neurosci 2010; 260: 499-506.

[63] Doherty JL, Owen MJ. Genomic insights into the overlap between psychiatric disorders: implications for research and clinical practice. Genome Med 2014; 6: 29.

Chapter 5: Diffusion Tensor Imaging Techniques: Insights into Alterations of White Matter Underlying Major Depression and Suicidal Behavior

CHAPTER 5

Diffusion Tensor Imaging Techniques: Insights into Alterations of White Matter Underlying Major Depression and Suicidal Behavior

Gianluca Serafini*, Matteo Respino, Martino Belvederi Murri and Mario Amore

Department of Neuroscience, Rehabilitation, Ophthalmology, Genetics, Maternal and Child Health (DINOGMI), Section of Psychiatry, University of Genoa, Genoa, Italy

Abstract: Based on diffusion tensor imaging (DTI) studies, brain white matter (WM) abnormalities have been recently suggested to play a critical role in the pathophysiology of major depressive disorder (MDD) and suicidal behavior. DTI studies reported the presence of altered WM integrity both in subjects with MDD and suicidal behavior. Microstructural WM abnormalities located in neural circuits critically involved in emotional processes and mood regulation may result in enhanced vulnerability to psychiatric morbidity contributing to functional impairments. However, the role and significance of WM alterations as well as their possible implications in patients with major affective disorders and suicidal behavior are still poorly understood. The present chapter aims to comprehensively review the current literature about the association between microstructural WM alterations as assessed by DTI techniques, MDD and suicide behavior.

Keywords: Diffusion tensor imaging techniques, Early-onset depression, Fractional anisotropy, Magnetic resonance images, Major depression, Microstructural white matter lesions, Mood disorders, Suicidal behavior.

INTRODUCTION

Major depressive disorder (MDD) is a common psychiatric condition associated with significant disability and psychosocial impairment. Research suggests that MDD is related with frequent recurrences, incomplete recovery between episodes, residual symptoms, poor psychosocial adjustment, and suicidal behavior [1, 2]. Suicide is a complex and multifaceted behavior aimed at self-destruction and associated with a relevant distress at the community level and among all individuals who are near the victim; however, suicide is a rare social event and its

***Corresponding author Gianluca Serafini:** Department of Neuroscience, Rehabilitation, Ophthalmology, Genetics, Maternal and Child Health (DINOGMI), Section of Psychiatry, University of Genoa, IRCCS San Martino, Largo Rosanna Benzi 10, 16132, Genoa, Italy; Tel: 00390103537668 (Off.), 00393475372316 (Mobile); Fax- 00390103537669; E-mail: gianluca.serafini@unige.it

Puneetpal Singh and Sarabjit Mastana (Eds)

prediction is quite difficult. Untreated unipolar MDD is one of the most important risk factor associated with completed suicide and it may account for at least 56-87% of the cases [2]. Suicidality may be significantly reduced after the clinical recovery [2] as suggested by the fact that it is a state- and severity-dependent behavior. The existence of clinical, psychological and psychosocial risk factors able to identify those individuals who are at high risk for suicide has been well recognized in clinical practice [3] but the mechanisms underlying this complex behavior as well as the link with psychopathology are currently unclear.

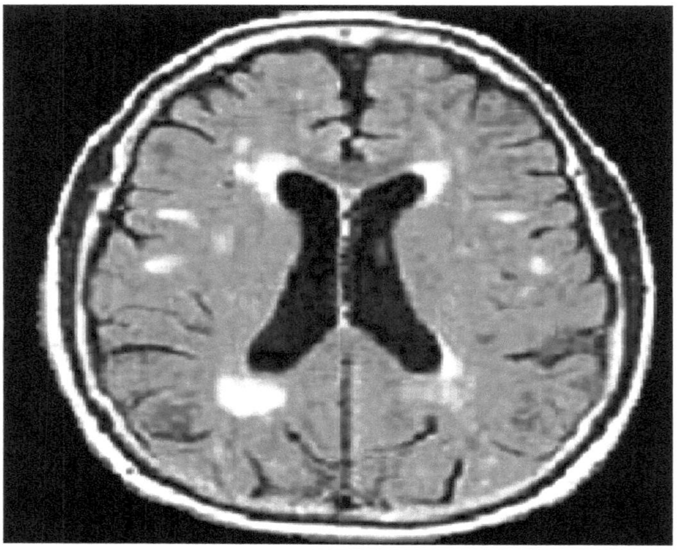

Fig. (1). White matter hyperintensities as assessed by MRI.
Note: White matter hyperintensities (WMHs) may be considered as hyperintense signals on T2-weighted magnetic resonance images (MRI) reflecting ependymal loss and differing degrees of myelination in the context of white matter. These lesions can be related to a variety of clinical conditions and pathophysiological processes. WMHs, depending on their main localization, are commonly classified as periventricular hyperintensities (PWMHs) or deep white matter hyperintensities (DWMHs) with the latter predominantly having a vascular origin.

White matter hyperintensities (WMHs) described as hyperintense signals on T2-weighted magnetic resonance images (MRI) are characterized by ependymal loss and differing degrees of myelination (Fig. **1**) in the brain [4, 5]. Based on their localization, they may be classified in periventricular WMHs and deep WMHs (usually associated with a vascular aetiology).

The presence of these aspecific brain WM lesions have been reported in adults with mood disorders and suicidal behavior, children and young adults [6-9] whereas they seem to be not common in patients with first episode psychosis [10].

Importantly, diffusion tensor imaging (DTI) studies may detect microstructural WM abnormalities with high special resolution and allow to investigate the integrity of WM tracts critically involved in mood regulation.

According to the current literature, several studies examined the association between WM abnormalities, MDD [11-30] and suicidal behavior [31-34] using DTI techniques (Fig. **2**). Taylor and colleagues [35] hypothesized that patients with WM lesions may be more likely to develop mood disorders and suicide because of possible disruption of neuroanatomic pathways. Mood regulation may be related to abnormal connections between several key brain structures such as the prefrontal cortex, amygdala, hippocampus, thalamus and basal ganglia [36]. Several subtypes of mood disorders ranging from sub-threshold affective temperament traits [37] to severe (psychotic and not psychotic) mood disorders [38-41] have been clinically described.

However, the association between microstructural WM abnormalities, affective temperaments and suicidal behavior in patients with MDD is poorly understood. Therefore, the present chapter is aimed to critically review the current literature about this association.

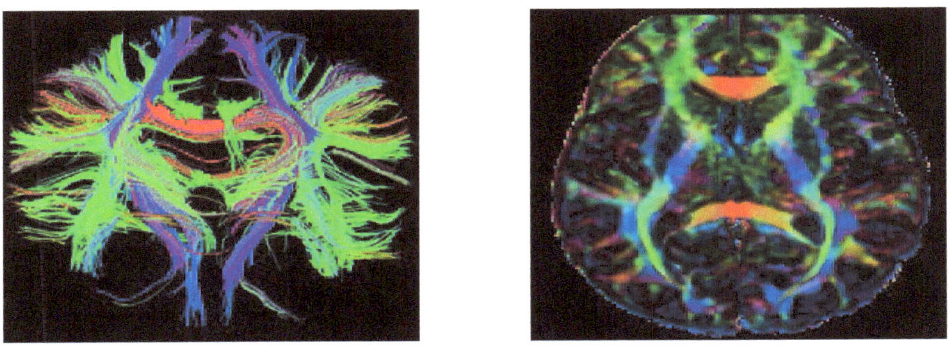

Fig. (2). Recent MRI techniques: DTI.
Note: During the recent years, most recent magnetic resonance techniques such as Diffusion Tensor Imaging (DTI) significantly contributed to improve our understanding of the role and significance of WM abnormalities in patients with major neuropsychiatric disorders. DTI may be used to investigate the three-dimensional diffusion properties of water throughout brain tissues.

METHODS

Information Sources, Search Strategy and Study Selection

A detailed search strategy was carried out in order to identify the most relevant studies investigating WM abnormalities detected by DTI in major affective disorders and suicidal behavior through Medline databases. In order to provide a new and timely comprehensive search of WM alterations and their possible involvement in MDD, we performed a detailed search in Pubmed/Medline to identify research published in English language during the period between January 2000 and January 2014.

The search used a combination of the following terms: ("Major depressive disorder" OR "MDD" OR "Major depression") AND ("Microstructural white matter lesions" OR "white matter abnormalities" OR "white matter changes signals") AND ("Diffusion Tensor Imaging") OR ("DTI"). The reference lists of publications selected for the possible inclusion were additionally investigated to find further relevant studies. Where a title/abstract seemed to focus on a study eligible for inclusion, the full-text article was carefully analyzed to evaluate its relevance based on the inclusion criteria. The present review chapter did not focus on samples of patients with bipolar depression or patients with treatment-resistant major depression. All English language full-text articles including original data about the main topic were selected.

Inclusion and Exclusion Criteria

Studies were included based on the following criteria: (a) being an original paper in a peer-reviewed journal, (b) including a clear analysis of the association between WM abnormalities and MDD using DTI techniques.

Recorded Variables

The recorded variables for each full-text article about WM abnormalities and MDD were as follows: study design, sample features, main findings, limitations and conclusions (for more details, see Tables **1-4**).

Number of Studies Selected

The main search strategy provided a total of one-hundred and sixty articles of which, after a complete analysis, seventy full-text articles were screened and ninety were excluded. Specifically, we excluded articles not published in peer reviewed journals and not in the English language, articles without abstracts, abstracts that did not explicitly mention the link between WM abnormalities and MDD, articles published before 2000 and those including unclear data about materials and methods, and/or number of patients analyzed. We initially evaluated forty-nine and then forty-three articles for eligibility but 6 full-text articles were further excluded due to the low-relevance to the main topic, leaving 37 articles that fulfilled our inclusion criteria.

Types of Studies Selected

Several DTI studies documented the association between WM abnormalities and MDD. Tables **1** and **2** summarize the most relevant findings that have been published about this association. During recent years, magnetic resonance techniques such as DTI largely contributed to a better understanding of the role and significance of WM abnormalities in patients with MDD. Here, the most relevant studies concerning the association between WM abnormalities based on their main brain location and MDD using DTI studies are reported as follows. The majority of these studies were cross-sectional in nature.

RESULTS

The Impact of Microstructural WM Brain Alterations as Assessed by DTI in Patients with MDD: Abnormalities of Prefrontal, Frontal, Temporal and Parietal Tracts

During recent years magnetic resonance techniques such as DTI largely contributed to a better understanding of the role and significance of WMHs in patients with MDD. Alexopoulos *et al.* reported in 2002 [42] for the first time the possible association between microstructural WM abnormalities such as a lower fractional anisotropy (FA) in frontal regions and a lower rate of remission in 13 patients with geriatric MDD. These abnormalities were described in the context of WM of right and left frontal regions, lateral to the anterior cingulated cortex. When compared to healthy controls, WM brain networks seem to be significantly impaired in subjects with MDD. There are evidence that these two groups can be distinguished based on the hubs of WM brain networks including superior frontal gyrus, left middle frontal gyrus, bilateral middle temporal gyrus and bilateral inferior temporal gyrus [11]. Microstructural alterations in WM integrity may be revealed very early in the course of disease. Li *et al.* [43] recently found prefrontal WM alterations in a group of 19 first-episode, treatment-naïve young adults with MDD. In a sample of 14 first-episode, treatment-naive young adult MDD young individuals with MDD, Ma *et al.* [44] found significantly reduced FA values involving WM of the right middle frontal gyrus, left lateral occipito-temporal gyrus and subgyral and angular gyri of the right parietal lobe. The authors also reported significantly reduced FA values involving the right superior frontal gyrus compared to healthy controls. One study reported a negative correlation between FA and activity levels involving the left primary motor cortex and left parahippocampal gyrus WM [45].

Ouyang *et al.* [46] compared subjects affected by major depression relative to control subjects. They found microstructural alterations in several WM areas as revealed by lower FA values in the bilateral medial frontal gyri, right subgyral frontal and temporal lobes and left middle frontal and cingulate gyri. A significant reduction in FA values of right parietal WM has also been reported among patients affected by major depression [28]. Moreover, the severity of depressive symptoms was associated with a decrease in FA values of mediodorsal and dorsolateral prefrontal cortex tracts and an increase in FA values of thalamic centromedian tracts. Lamar *et al.* [47] reported an association between WM alterations and severity of depressive symptoms in 79 euthymic older adults assessed for cognitive and depressive symptoms, vascular global burden and DTI analysis for WM microstructure. Major depression in the elderly seems to be closely related to WM alterations of the frontal regions. Nobuhara *et al.* [48] investigated a group of late-life depressed patients and reported lower FA of the frontal and temporal lobes characterized by a negative association between severity of depression and reduction in FA values of the inferior frontal region. Taylor *et al.* [48] reported that microstructural changes in the WM of the right superior frontal gyrus are associated with Late-Life Depression (LLD). Specifically, even after controlling for age, sex, hypertension and heart disease, significantly lower FA values were found in the right superior frontal gyrus WM of depressed patients compared to controls.

Furthermore, when compared to healthy controls Nobuhara *et al.* reported frontal and temporal FA reductions in a sample of subjects affected by LLD after ECT treatments [49]. Finally, after left repetitive transcranial magnetic stimulation (rTMS), Kozel and colleagues using DTI techniques performed before and after 4 to 6 weeks of daily rTMS treatments found a non-significant change in the left prefrontal WM of depressed patients [50].

DTI Studies Reporting WM Abnormalities of Cortical-Subcortical Neural Circuits in MDD

Cortical-subcortical neural circuits seem to be impaired in MDD and WM integrity alterations may play a central role in this structural impairment. In a very limited sample of drug-free patients affected by MDD, some authors [25] reported clusters of FA reduction in WM brain regions such as bilateral frontal WM, anterior limbs of internal capsule, cerebellum, left putamen and right thalamus. In another study on drug-free young adult depressed subjects at their first major depressive episode [51], a decrease has been reported in FA values in the left WM anterior limb of the internal capsule, right parahippocampal gyrus, and left posterior cingulate cortex relative to healthy controls. Moreover, the same authors found a negative correlation between depression severity and FA values in the left anterior limb of the internal capsule (ALIC). Among MDD patients and relative to controls, results derived by another study showed lower FA values in the left hemisphere including ALIC and inferior parietal portion of the superior longitudinal fasciculus [52].

Alexopoulos *et al.* [53] compared patients who remitted from depressive symptoms and patients who did not remit after treatment and reported a reduction in FA values of multiple frontal limbic brain areas in non-remitted group. Furthermore, the association between WM microstructural abnormalities and depressive symptoms has been widely confirmed among MDD patients relative to controls in several meta-analyses [29, 54] reporting a reduction of FA in WM integrity of superior longitudinal fasciculus and tracts connecting the prefrontal cortex to other cortical (frontal, temporal and occipital lobes) and subcortical areas (amygdala and hippocampus) as well as an increase in FA values of the fronto-occipital fasciculus.

Guo *et al.* [55] reported lower FA values in the bilateral internal capsule, the bilateral anterior corona radiate and the right external capsule in adult depressed subjects. Korgaonkar *et al.* [15] analyzed structural connectivity in MDD outpatients relative to a group of 102 healthy controls reporting lowered structural connectivity in patients affected by MDD within two distinct brain networks: the default-mode network and the frontal-thalamus-caudate regions. The authors suggested that connectivity alterations between nodes in these areas may represent critical neurobiological characteristics associated with MDD.

Furthermore, major brainstem WM tracts and their activity in MDD have been investigated with the probabilistic tractography of DTI among depressed subjects and healthy controls [16]. A significant and specific reduction in WM integrity of the solitary tract connecting brainstem to amygdala has been reported. Finally, in similar studies other authors [24, 56] reported significantly lower FA values in frontal lobe, bilateral anterior/posterior limbs of the internal capsules, left external capsule, right thalamic radiation and left inferior longitudinal fasciculus and frontolimbic neural pathways. Results derived by a study comparing a sample of patients affected by MDD with melancholic features with a group of healthy controls showed a decrease in FA values of several WM connections such as the tract between right ventral tegmental area and the lateral orbitofrontal cortex or the tract between the ventral tegmental area and dorsolateral orbitofrontal cortex

[26]. Depression severity also appeared negatively correlated with FA in the same WM connections.

WM microstructure in patients affected by depression with melancholic features has also been investigated by Korgaonkar *et al.* [57] after conducting a tract-based spatial statistics analysis comparing subjects affected by MDD with melancholic features and healthy controls. When compared with controls, WM association fibers of melancholic patients such as those in limbic system, dorsolateral prefrontal cortex, thalamus and corpus callosum did show an average 7.8% lower FA value associated with decreased axial and increased radial diffusivity, respectively. Based on these findings, the authors postulated the existence of a pattern of reduced myelination or other degenerative changes in the mentioned WM regions. Using 3T scanner and DTI techniques, Colloby *et al.* [58] investigated the integrity of WM tracts in subjects with LLD relative to healthy controls and reported that compared to healthy individuals, patients with LLD showed lower FA in frontal, temporal and midbrain regions, suggesting that an impairment of limbic-orbitofrontal networks may play a critical role in the pathogenesis of LLD.

Some authors suggested a role of electroconvulsive therapy (ECT) as a modulator of WM abnormalities in fronto-limbic areas [17]. The authors found a significant increase in FA values of dorsal fronto-limbic circuits encompassing the anterior cingulum, forceps minor and left superior longitudinal fasciculus in patients receiving ECT compared to controls. In addition, the authors reported reductions in radial and mean diffusivity of the anterior thalamic radiation related to therapeutic response and suggested that altered WM microstructure in pathways connecting frontal and limbic areas occurring in MDD were modulated by ECT and related to therapeutic response. DTI techniques were performed in a group of depressed subjects before and after four-week guided imagery psychotherapy as well as in a healthy control comparison group [30]. Depressed patients demonstrated significantly increased FA values in the right thalamus.

Abnormalities of Cortico-Cortical Motor Pathways as Assessed by DTI in MDD

Bracht *et al.* [27] investigated structural connectivity and motor activity of WM cortico-cortical motor pathways in depressed subjects who underwent DTI and 24 hour actigraphy. Activity level and mean diffusivity in the left dorsolateral prefrontal cortex- pre-supplementary motor area tract were negatively correlated among MDD patients when compared with controls. Furthermore, depressed patients demonstrated a reduction in activity levels as well as an increase in mean diffusivity in pathways linking left pre-supplementary motor area with supplementary motor area and right supplementary motor area with primary motor cortex.

Abnormalities of Anterior and Posterior Cingulum Tracts as Assessed by DTI in MDD

Bae and colleagues [59] suggested a significant decrease in FA values involving right anterior cingulate cortex, bilateral superior frontal gyri and left middle frontal gyrus in patients with LLD. Also, anterior cingulated-limbic WM alterations seem to play an important contribution in explaining depression severity and treatment outcomes. In a group of depressed patients who completed an 8-week antidepressant treatment, Korgaonkar *et al.* [14] reported the relevance of abnormalities within anterior cingulate-limbic WM in predicting antidepressant treatment outcome. Moreover, Hayakama *et al.* [22] reported a positive correlation between symptoms severity scores (as measured by Center for Epidemiologic Studies Depression Scale) and radial diffusivity in the right anterior cingulum women affected by subclinical depression when compared to healthy controls.

In addition, WM integrity in adolescent depression has been preliminary evaluated in MDD subjects compared with healthy controls [23], suggesting alterations among depressed adolescents in the anterior cingulum and anterior corona radiate. In this study, a negative correlation between severity of depressive symptoms and WM integrity in the genu of corpus callosum, anterior thalamic radiation, anterior cingulum and sagittal stratum has also been reported. Concerning response or remission to pharmacological treatments and DTI studies, Taylor and colleagues [59] reported an increase of FA values in the superior frontal gyri and anterior cingulate cortices bilaterally in a group of responders to sertraline; however, they did not show significant associations between apparent diffusion coefficient measures and remission.

Relative to healthy controls, lower activity levels in frontal WM areas and posterior cingulum among MDD patients have been demonstrated by Walther *et al.* [45].

Abnormalities of Superior and Inferior Longitudinal Fasciculi as Assessed by DTI in MDD

A recent study [12] on patients with MDD found lower FA values in the left superior longitudinal fasciculus and in the right anterior thalamic radiation together with an increased radial diffusivity values in the bilateral superior longitudinal fasciculus and decreased axial diffusivity values in the bilateral anterior thalamic radiation. Negative associations between FA values and depression or illness duration have been suggested to involve respectively the superior longitudinal fasciculus and the anterior thalamic radiation. Another study compared drug-free first-episode depressed patients and healthy controls and revealed lower FA values in the right superior longitudinal fasciculus within the frontal lobe, right middle frontal and left parietal WM [60].

Abnormalities of Uncinate Fasciculus

WM brain alterations may be also observed in adolescent MDD samples. A DTI study showed that depression in adolescence was characterized by lower FA and higher radial diffusivity in the uncinate fasciculus, bilaterally [13]. de Kwaasteniet *et al.* [20] reported impairments of WM integrity within the uncinate fasciculus in MDD subjects when compared with healthy subjects. Moreover, in the MDD group the integrity of uncinate fasciculus and subgenual anterior cingulate cortex functional connectivity negatively correlated with the bilateral hippocampus. The integrity of uncinate fasciculus has been investigated in several studies among patients with MDD. In the study of Zhang *et al.* [61], the authors reported a negative correlation between severity of depressive symptoms and normalized number of fibers within the right uncinate fasciculus. In a combined DTI-fMRI resting state study [55], FA of the left uncinate fasciculus resulted significantly associated with functional connectivity between the left ventrolateral prefrontal cortex/left amygdala and left ventrolateral prefrontal cortex/left hippocampus among MDD older subjects. The authors also found a negative correlation between left uncinate fasciculus FA and left ventromedial prefrontal cortex/caudate functional connectivity. In addition, among MDD patients, a failure to achieve remission has recently been associated with a reduction in FA values of the medial body of the fornix [18].

Abnormalities within the Corpus Callusum

Lower WM FA values have been found in limbic-cortical-striatal-thalamic circuit, corpus callosum and anterior-superior corona radiata based on tract-based spatial statistics findings [13].

Guo *et al.* [55] found that the genu of corpus callosum showed lower FA values in adult depressed subjects compared to healthy controls. Tract-based spatial statistics (TBSS) have been used to examine WM microstructure in treatment-naive adolescents with clinical depression and controls [62]. Whole-brain analysis revealed lower FA values and an increase in radial and mean diffusivity in the body of corpus callosum whereas results from a region-of-interest (ROI) analysis showed higher FA values in the uncinate fasciculus and increased axial-reduced radial diffusivity.

Recently, a relevant decrease in WM integrity of the corpus callosum has been demonstrated in MDD patients [63]. In this study, WM integrity of the corpus callosum also related negatively with worsening of depressive symptoms and a reduction of WM integrity has been demonstrated in superior longitudinal fasciculus and anterior corona radiata.

Studies that did not Support the Association Between WM Abnormalities and MDD

Some studies did not report significant WM microstructure differences between healthy and depressed subjects. Choi *et al.* [19] did not find significant differences in WM FA values and radial, mean or axonal diffusivity in drug-free depressed individuals assessed with voxel-based morphometry or DTI. Furthermore, no significant differences in WM microstructure were reported by Bezerra *et al.* [64] in a group of late-life mild to moderate depressed subjects relative to healthy controls. An additional study comparing MDD patients and controls [65] revealed no significant difference between both groups in terms of FA and WM volume of the entire brain although only a trend for a negative correlation between FA and total days of depression was reported in right anterior cingulate. Finally, only a trend for reduction in FA values in the left sagittal stratum and reduced FA in the right cingulate cortex/posterior body of corpus callosum was found by Kieseppä *et al.* [66] in depressed patients relative to controls.

The studies of Steffens *et al.* [67] and Bae *et al.* [68] have been not reported throughout the main main text but were regularly reported within Table **1**.

Table 1. Most relevant studies about the association between WM abnormalities and MDD using DTI studies.

Study Design	Sample	Main Results	Limitations	Conclusion	Reference
Cross-sectional	59 subjects (30 MDD, 29 HC)	Hubs (bilateral dorsolateral part of superior frontal gyrus, left middle frontal gyrus,	Cross-sectional study design, small sample size	Aberrant hubs of the frontal-parieto circuit were related to MDD. They might	Qin *et al.* [11]

Table 1: contd…

Study Design	Sample	Main Results	Limitations	Conclusion	Reference
		bilateral middle temporal gyrus, bilateral inferior temporal gyrus) distinguished subjects with depression and HC with an accuracy of 83.05%.		be identified as potential markers to recognize depressed patients.	
Cross-sectional	73 subjects (44 MDD, 27 HC)	MDD patients had significantly lower FA values than controls, for the SLF and ATR. Lower FA values were reported in combination with elevated RD values in the bilateral SLF and lower AD values in the bilateral ATR. FA values were negatively correlated with the severity of depressive symptoms in the SLF and illness duration in the right SLF and ATR.	Cross-sectional design, limited sample size. The study did not carry out tractography and suffers from limited directional resolution of the suboptimal DTI protocol (30 directions). Another caveat is the later-on bipolar disorder diagnosis of first-episode MDD.	Significant alterations may occur in the WM micro-integrity of the left SLF and right ATR in MDD patients relative to HC.	Lai and Wu [12]
Cross-sectional	94 subjects (52 unmedicated adolescents with MDD and 42 HC)	MDD patients had significantly lower FA and higher RD in bilateral UF. No significant differences were observed in the cingulum. TBSS results revealed lower FA values in the limbic-cortical-striatal-thalamic circuit WM tracts, corpus callosum, and anterior and superior corona radiata WM.	Cross-sectional study design. Subjects with anxiety were not excluded in the subanalyses. The use of a non-isotropic voxel size in DTI scans is more likely to lead to an underestimation of FA values in tracts in which there are crossing fibers.	Unmedicated adolescent depression is associated with lower FA in emotion regulatory networks, which may underlie the functional frontolimbic differences in depressive disorders. Lower FA in the UF could be a predisposing risk factor in depression.	LeWinn *et al.* [13]

Table 1: contd…

Study Design	Sample	Main Results	Limitations	Conclusion	Reference
8 weeks follow-up after a randomized AD treatment	102 MDD outpatients (74 at follow-up) and 34 age- and gender-matched HC	The stria terminalis FA and cingulate FA were shown to predict remission with an overall accuracy of 62%, a sensitivity of 56% and a specificity of 68%. When age was added to this model, improved prediction accuracy overall to 74%, with a sensitivity of 74% and a specificity of 75% were obtained.	The generalization of the main findings is difficult, and the study did not carry out DTI tractography analyses;	Anterior cingulate-limbic WM is a predictor of AD treatment outcome in MDD.	Korgaonkar *et al.* [14]
Cross-sectional	95 MDD outpatients and 102 HC	The study found lower structural connectivity within two distinct brain networks among MDD patients: the first involves the regions of the default mode network and the second the frontal cortex, thalamus, and caudate regions that are central in emotional and cognitive processes. These two altered networks were observed in the context of an overall preservation of topology.	The potential for DTI tractography to generate false positives and false negatives in tract reconstruction cannot be excluded.	Alterations in structural connectivity between nodes of the default mode network and the frontal-thalamo-caudate regions are fundamental neurobiological characteristics associated with MDD.	Korgaonkar *et al.* [15]
Cross-sectional	95 MDD patients and 34 age- and gender-matched HC	Lower WM integrity was found in the RST ($p<0.009$ independent t-test) among MDD patients relative to HC. Also, no association	The study used mean FA for the whole tract that may cause a dilution of signal from the more subtle structural abnormalities. The EPI-related	Results provide evidence of alterations in WM structural connectivity between brainstem and amygdala and loss of WM	Song *et al.* [16]

Table 1: contd…

Study Design	Sample	Main Results	Limitations	Conclusion	Reference
		between severity of depressive symptoms and the decrease in WM integrity was reported.	geometric distortion and local sensitivity loss due to signal drop out cannot be excluded.	integrity in the RST among MDD patients supporting the theory that altered brainstem-amygdala connectivity may impact on MDD circuits.	
Cross-sectional	18 MDD subjects and 24 HC	WM integrity of the UF was reduced and FC between subgenual ACC and MTL was enhanced in MDD. MDD patients did show a negative correlation between UF integrity and subgenual ACC FC with bilateral hippocampi; this negative structure-function relation in MDD was positively associated with depression severity.	The small sample size and cross-sectional study design are major limitations. The use of psychotropic medication in seven MDD subjects is another shortcoming.	Structural abnormalities in MDD associated with increased FC between subgenual ACC and MTL are concomitant with severity of depressive symptoms and may contribute to increased FC within the frontolimbic network.	de Kwaasteniet *et al.* [20]
Cross-sectional	21 subjects with subclinical depression and 21 matched HC	The volumes of both anterior cingulate gyri and the right rectal gyrus were smaller in subclinically depressed women than in HC. CES-D score and RD in the right anterior cingulum of subclinically depressed women were positively correlated.	The small sample size is a major limitation.	GM volume reduction and WM integrity change in specific frontal brain areas may be associated with depressive symptoms in women, even at a subclinical level	Hayakawa *et al.* [22]
Cross-sectional	17 medication-free adolescents with depression and 16 matched	A lower WM integrity in adolescents with MDD relative to	Small sample size and very liberal thresholds were used for the	A general pattern of impaired WM integrity was found in the	Henderson *et al.* [23]

Table 1: contd...

Study Design	Sample	Main Results	Limitations	Conclusion	Reference
	HC	HC in the anterior cingulum and anterior corona radiate was found. Among MDD patients, severity of depressive symptoms was correlated with a decrease in WM integrity in the genu of corpus callosum, anterior thalamic radiation, anterior cingulum, and sagittal stratum. Anhedonia and irritability were associated with WM microstructural abnormalities. Anhedonia was associated with alterations in reward processing WM network whereas irritability was associated with lower FA integrity in the sagittal stratum, anterior corona radiata, and tracts leading to prefrontal and temporal cortices.	analyses. Another limitation is the inability to correct for multiple comparisons.	depressed adolescents. MDD could be characterized by a disconnection in prefrontal and limbic networks, and distinct WM tracts abnormalities could be associated with specific clinical symptoms.	
Cross-sectional	31 MDD adolescent patients and 31 demographically-matched HC	WM FA abnormalities were found in the CC genu, internal and external capsule tracts, thalamus, and midbrain.	MDD illness duration was not assessed and the sample had a highly variable AD treatment history. A third of the recruited subjects had comorbid anxiety.	WM abnormal connections of the frontal lobe in MDD adolescents might represent important markers of early-life onset depression.	Bessette *et al.* [24]
Cross-sectional	19 drug-free MDD patients and 19 age-matched HC	Lower FA values were observed in the bilateral frontal WM, the anterior	Small sample size. Also, the correction for eddy current-induced	The present findings suggested WM integrity	Tha *et al.* [25]

Table 1: contd…

Study Design	Sample	Main Results	Limitations	Conclusion	Reference
		limbs of the internal capsule, the left putamen, the mediodorsal nucleus of the right thalamus, and the anterior and superior aspect of bilateral cerebellar hemispheres of the patients, also if controlled for age and gender. The peak position of the FA histograms of the patients was significantly lower than that of HC. A moderate to positive correlation with the total disease duration and the duration of the current disease episode was found. FA values of the left cerebellar hemisphere revealed a moderate positive correlation with age. There was no significant difference in the regional FA values or in the peak positions of FA histograms between the gender groups.	distortion was not performed. The slice thickness used for DTI was 5 mm, and the interslice gap was 1.5 mm - ideally, thinner slices without interslice gap are destre. DSM-IV-TR was used to diagnose MDD among patients whereas MINI was used to exclude psychiatric diseases among HC. Potential bias arising from the use of different diagnostic assessment methods cannot be excluded.	abnormalities of the frontal-subcortical circuits and cerebro-cerebellar tracts.	
Cross-sectional	22 MDD patients (12 melancholic, 10 non-melancholic) and 21 HC	Mean-FA did not differ between HC and MDD patients. Melancholic MDD-patients had reduced mean-FA in right VTA-lOFC and VTA-dlPFC connections when compared to HC.	The small sample size did not allow the generalization of findings. These are preliminary data from group comparison between melancholic and non-melancholic	The melancholic subtype of MDD seems to be characterized by WM abnormalities of the MFB. WM microstructure abnormalities are associated with	Bracht *et al.* [26]

Table 1: contd…

Study Design	Sample	Main Results	Limitations	Conclusion	Reference
		Melancholic MDD-patients did show lower mean-FA than non-melancholic MDD-patients in the right VTA-lOFC connection. Mean-FA of these pathways correlated negatively with depression scale rating scores.	MDD patients due to small sample size and heterogeneous age.	both depression severity and anhedonia.	
Cross-sectional	21 MDD patients and 21 matched HC	Patients had lower AL and showed increased MD in pathways linking left pre-SMA and SMA-proper, and right SMA-proper and M1. Exploratory analyses showed a positive association of AL and mean-FA in the right rACCpre-SMA connection in MDD. Only MDD patients with lower AL had a negative linear association of AL and mean-MD in the left DLPFC-pre-SMA connection.	All MDD patients were medicated; it was not possible to rule out the impact of medication on AL. Among MDD patients medication might have influenced WM microstructure. Analysis of the association between WM integrity of motor pathways and AL did not survive to the correction for multiple comparisons.	The pathways connecting motor cortices with the basal ganglia system do not seem to directly contribute to psychomotor retardation in MDD. Abnormal WM organisation of rACC-pre-SMA and DLPFC-pre-SMA pathways may contribute to movement initiation in MDD.	Bracht *et al.* [27]
Cross-sectional	20 MDD patients and 20 matched HC	According to a whole brain analysis, FA deficits were only found in right parietal WM whereas a positive correlation was reported between increased thalamic FA and severity of symptoms. Mediodorsal to	The specificity of the TOI approach, the heterogenous and small sample were the most relevant limitations.	Among MDD patients, a robust parietal FA reduction controlled for age effects, and subcortical disease state dependency of FA in thalamic tracts was found.	Osoba *et al.* [28]

Table 1: contd…

Study Design	Sample	Main Results	Limitations	Conclusion	Reference
		dorsolateral prefrontal cortex (DLPFC) were reduced in FA and a further reduction between mediodorsal and centromedian thalamic tracts towards amygdala were paralleled by primary amygdala FA decrease.			
Meta-analysis	11 studies (combined sample of 231 patients with MDD and 261 comparison participants)	Four consistent WM locations of reduced FA in patients with MDD: right frontal lobe, right fusiform gyrus, left frontal lobe, and right occipital lobe. The main fascicles involved were the right inferior longitudinal fasciculus, right inferior fronto-occipital fasciculus, right posterior thalamic radiation and interhemispheric fibres running through the genu and body of the corpus callosum.	The relatively small number of studies included and the heterogeneity of DTI data acquisition and analysis were the most relevant limitations.	VBA of DTI studies including MDD patients consistently identified decreased in WM FA of the tracts linking the prefrontal cortex within cortical (frontal, temporal and occipital lobes) and subcortical areas (amygdala and hippocampus).	Liao *et al.* [29]
Cross-sectional	24 unipolar MDD older subjects in phase of remission	Positive correlations between left UF FA and rsFC between the left ventrolateral PFC and the left amygdala and between the left ventrolateral PFC and the left	The study did not include non-depressed older controls and the small sample size limits the generalization of findings. Also, left-sides findings were not sufficiently	Geriatric depression can be associated with decreased structural integrity of WM tracts in the prefrontal cortex.	Steffens *et al.* [67]

Table 1: contd…

Study Design	Sample	Main Results	Limitations	Conclusion	Reference
		hippocampus were reported. A significant negative correlation between left ventromedial PFC-caudate rsFC and left UF FA was also observed.	investigated.		
Cross-sectional	19 first-episode young adults MDD patients and 20 matched HC	MDD patients showed a significant reduction in FA values throughout the prefrontal WM.	Major limitations are: the small sample size, large range of illness course (from 3 to 24 months), the absence of ADC and possible type I errors (uncorrected).	WM prefrontal abnormalities may occur early in the course of MDD and may be related to the neuropathology of depression during lifespan.	Li *et al.* [43]
Cross-sectional	14 first-episode, treatment-naive young adult MDD patients and 14 HC	Lower FA values among MDD group compared to HC in the WM of the right middle frontal gyrus, left lateral occipitotemporal gyrus, subgyral and angular gyri of the right parietal lobe were found.	The small sample size did not allow the generalization of findings.	WM microstructural alterations could be present early in the course of illness. Findings also supported the hypothesis that WM lesions may disrupt critical networks involved in mood regulation contributing to MDD.	Ma *et al.* [44]
Cross-sectional	13 LLD patients and 13 matched HC	Among LLD patients, lower FA values of widespread regions of the frontal and temporal lobes were found. FA values of the inferior frontal brain region were inversely associated with the severity of depressive symptoms.	The small and selected sample size and multiple tests for correlations between the degree of WM macrostructural abnormalities and clinical symptom severity were major limitations. Also, the study did not investigate the effects of AD on DTI measures.	The orbitofrontal networks seem to be related to symptom severity in LLD.	Nobuhara *et al.* [49]

Table 1: contd…

Study Design	Sample	Main Results	Limitations	Conclusion	Reference
Cross-sectional	106 LLD and 84 HC	LLD patients had significantly lower FA values in the right ACC, bilateral superior frontal gyri, and left middle frontal gyrus WM even after controlling for covariates.	Major limitations are: the cross-sectional study design and the lack of specificity of the findings for the dorsolateral prefrontal and anterior cingulate circuits (due to ROI analyses).	A reduction in FA is observed in subjects with LLD throughout the DLPFC and right ACC. Altered connectivity between brain regions is involved in the pathophysiology of depression.	Bae *et al.* [68]
Cross-sectional	79 euthymic older adults	GDS-15 correlated with DTI measures of MD and FA but only approached significance for T2-weighted MRI measures of WMH. After adjusting for factors known to influence the development of WMH and depression, indices of WM integrity remained significantly associated with GDS-15 scores. Only DTI-derived measures of WM integrity contributed to the variance in GDS-15 scores after logistical regression analyses.	The sample size is limited to euthymic older adults. Also, some of participants may have had undisclosed psychiatric conditions or undetected cognitive impairment.	WM impairment is associated with the endorsement of depressive symptoms in euthymic older adults. DTI may be more sensitive to this damage when compared with T2-WMH.	Lamar *et al.* [47]
Cross-sectional	21 MDD patients and 21 age-matched HC	Significantly lower FA and increased RD of the right UF were observed in MDD patients relative to HC. Among MDD subjects, depression severity	The relatively small sample size together with the cross-sectional study design did not allow the generalization of findings.	WM microstructural alterations of the right UF may be found in patients with MDD. Severity of depressive symptoms is	Zhang *et al.* [61]

Table 1: contd…

Study Design	Sample	Main Results	Limitations	Conclusion	Reference
		had a significant negative correlation with NNF in the right UF. Significant age effect (old<young) in HC group and laterality effect (L>R) in both groups in the FA values of the CB were found.		associated with reduced NNF in the right UF of MDD patients group.	
Cross-sectional	22 patients with treatment-responsive MDD and 19 well-matched HC	Four brain WM tracts with lower FA (*e.g.*, bilateral internal capsule, the genu of corpus callosum, the bilateral anterior corona radiata, and the right external capsule) have been identified in patients relative to healthy subjects.	The study included heterogeneous pharmacological profiles among treatment-responsive patients. Also, patients who were non-responsive to treatment were not included.	Alterations of WM tracts, in particular in the projection fibers and corpus callosum, may contribute to the pathogenesis of treatment-responsive MDD.	Guo *et al.* [55]
Cross-sectional	25 treatment-naïve depressed adolescents and 21 HC	Whole-brain analyses revealed that patients had a decrease in FA values in the body of CC, coupled with elevated RD and MD, and preserved AD. ROI analyses revealed that patients had higher FA values in the UF coupled with elevated AD, reduced RD and preserved MD.	The cross-sectional study design and the small sample size of adolescent males did not allow for an adequate test of an age×gender interaction effect on depressive symptoms. It was not possible to examine age-related changes in FA. Co-occurrence with anxiety was reported in most patients.	WM alterations within networks facilitating cognitive and emotional functioning are involved in the pathophysiology of MDD. These WM abnormalities are present early during the course of the disease.	Aghajani *et al.* [62]
Cross-sectional	14 adolescents affected by MDD and 14 HC	Adolescents with MDD showed a reduction in FA in the WM pathway	Most of the participants with MDD were under pharmacological	The study suggests that the pathophysiology of adolescent	Cullen *et al.* [56]

Table 1: contd…

Study Design	Sample	Main Results	Limitations	Conclusion	Reference
		connecting subgenual ACC to amygdala in the right hemisphere. Voxel-wise comparison of FA showed ten clusters where adolescents with MDD had significantly lower (uncorrected) FA than HC group within WM tracts including right and left uncinate and supragenual cingulum.	treatment. Also, the study included subjects with anxiety disorder as comorbid condition.	MDD involves abnormal fronto-limbic neural network. Findings provide evidence for reduced integrity in the WM tract connecting subgenual ACC to amygdala in patients group.	
Cross-sectional	29 nongeriatric MDD patients (11 with melancholia) and 39 HC	Relative to HC group, significant WM integrity deficits were observed only for the melancholic MDD subjects who also demonstrated a mean reduction of 7.8% in FA over WM regions associated with the limbic system, dorsolateral prefrontal cortex, thalamic projection fibers, CC, and other association fibers. Moreover, FA deficits were also associated with reduced axial and increased RD in these WM regions.	The study is cross-sectional in nature and is limited by the inability to ascertain the precise architecture of the involved tracts after their identification. The wide age difference between HC and melancholic MDD subgroup is another caveat.	The hypothesis concerning limbic-dorsolateral prefrontal cortex-thalamic dysfunction in MDD has been confirmed. These deficits are most prominent among melancholic MDD individuals.	Korgaonkar *et al.* [57]
Cross-sectional	21 MDD patients and 21 matched HC	Lower AL in MDD relative to HC was found. Different FA values between groups in frontal WM regions and	The study did not control for past special training (*e.g.*, learning to play music instruments). DTI data and analyses	Motor activity in MDD and HC is associated with WM integrity in motor circuits of the prefrontal cortex.	Walther *et al.* [45]

Table 1: contd…

Study Design	Sample	Main Results	Limitations	Conclusion	Reference
		the posterior cingulum were also reported. AL was positively associated with WM integrity in two clusters within the motor system and a positive association between FA and AL in HC WM underneath the right dorsal premotor cortex was reported. Only MDD patients revealed a positive association with the posterior cingulum and MDD patients showed a negative association between FA and AL underneath the left primary motor cortex and within the WM of left parahippocampal gyrus.	did not allow to identify the direction of single fibers. Some of the clusters detected appeared small. Finally, the use of medication is a potential confounder.	WM microstructure abnormalities in MDD are related to different motor behavior (*e.g.*, impaired motor planning and slowed gait).	
Cross-sectional	66 MDD patients and 66 matched HC	When compared to HC, MDD patients did show widespread regions of lower WM integrity, including regions throughout the CC, SLF, and anterior corona radiata. Symptom severity was negatively correlated with WM integrity, predominantly in the CC.	The cross-sectional design of the study is a major limitation. Also, the use of TBSS determined the exclusion of potentially interesting regions of peripheral WM.	MDD patients demonstrated widespread disruptions in the CC and SLF. It was found a correlation between increased depressive symptom severity and reduced WM integrity suggesting that WM abnormalities emerge mainly in those with a greater current illness burden.	Cole *et al.* [63]

Table 1: contd…

Study Design	Sample	Main Results	Limitations	Conclusion	Reference
Cross-sectional	38 patients affected by LLD and 30 matched HC	Compared to HC, patients with LLD showed lower FA in frontal, temporal and midbrain regions. Using corrected maps, no significant differences were observed in FA and MD parameters among LLD patients. Regression analyses revealed no significant relationship between DTI parameters and current depression.	The relatively small study sample did not allow the generalization of findings. TBSS determined the exclusion of potentially interesting regions of peripheral WM. Results did not survive to control for multiple comparisons.	Impairment of limbic-orbitofrontal networks may play a critical role in the pathogenesis of LLD.	Colloby *et al.* [58]
Cross-sectional	23 single-episode, medication-naive MDD and 21 HC	Compared to HC group, MDD patients had lower FA values in the right SLF within the frontal lobe, right middle frontal WM, and left inferior parietal lobe. MDD group had higher ADC in the right SLF within the frontal lobe, right middle frontal WM and left inferior parietal lobe.	The relatively small sample size did not allow the generalization of findings. Also, whether the analyses were carried out with false discovery rate whole brain corrected, no significant difference could be detected between the two groups.	Abnormalities in SLF, middle frontal and parietal WM in the early stage of MDD may play a critical role in the pathophysiology of MDD.	Wu *et al.* [60]
Cross-sectional	18 MDD treatment-naïve adult patients and 18 matched HC	When compared to HC, MDD patients had lower FA values in the bilateral medial frontal gyri, right subgyral frontal and temporal lobes, and left middle frontal and cingulate gyri; no	The small sample size together with cross-sectional study design and relatively limited cognitive assessment did not allow the generalization of findings.	WM integrity deficits in the fronto-limbic system is a significant substrate of MDD.	Ouyang *et al.* [46]

Table 1: contd...

Study Design	Sample	Main Results	Limitations	Conclusion	Reference
		correlation between mean FA values and cognitive scores was found.			
Cross-sectional	25 first-episode young-adult MDD patients and 25 matched HC	Relative to HC, MDD patients showed lower FA values in the left anterior limb of the internal capsule, right parahippocampal gyrus, and left posterior cingulate cortex. FA values in the left anterior limb of the internal capsule were negatively correlated with the severity of MDD symptoms.	The small sample size did not allow the generalization of findings. The study did not directly explore age-related changes in FA values due to the cross-sectional design and patients young age.	Alterations in WM integrity, especially those concerning the cortical-subcortical network, may contribute to the pathophysiology of MDD.	Zhu *et al.* [51]
Cross-sectional	45 MDD patients and 45 matched HC	Significantly lower FA in the left hemisphere (the anterior limb of the internal capsule and inferior parietal portion of the superior longitudinal fasciculus) was found among MDD patients compared to HC. A negative correlation between DTI measures in the left anterior limb of the internal capsule and severity of depression was found even after control for age and sex.	The cross-sectional study design and large range in ages among recruited individuals together with the cumulative duration of illness are major limitations.	Findings supported the hypothesis that the disruption of cortical-subcortical circuit integrity may be involved in the aetiology of MDD.	Zou *et al.* [52]
Cross-sectional DTI scans after 12	25 MDD patients who achieved remission and 23 MDD patients	Individuals who failed to achieve remission had lower FA in the	Major limitations are: the subject selection bias inherent to	Lower FA in distributed cerebral networks is associated with	Alexopoulos *et al.* [53]

Table 1: contd…

Study Design	Sample	Main Results	Limitations	Conclusion	Reference
weeks of AD treatment	who did not achieved remission	rostral and dorsal anterior cingulate, dorsolateral prefrontal cortex, genu of the CC, WM adjacent to the hippocampus, multiple posterior cingulate cortex regions, and insular WM relative to those who achieved remission. Lower FA was detected in the neostriatum and midbrain as well as select temporal and parietal regions.	imaging studies; lack of a placebo comparison group; fixed dose of the antidepressant; limited assessment of cognitive functions; and absence of long-term follow-up.	poor antidepressant response of geriatric depression and may represent a neuro-anatomical substrate predisposing to this disorder.	
Meta-analysis	7 studies (combined sample of 188 MDD patients and 221 HC).	MDD patients demonstrated reduced in FA values in the SLF and higher FA values in the fronto-occipital fasciculus compared to controls. Reduced FA in the left SLF was very stable with increases in the right fronto-occipital fasciculus (suggested by just one study).	The study suffers from the difficulty to distinguish the effects of illness duration from the effects of illness severity in this sample.	Significant reduction in FA values of the left SLF may play a key role in the pathophysiology of MDD.	Murphy and Frodl [54]
Cross-sectional	17 LLD subjects and 16 elderly HC	Relative to HC, depressed patients had lower FA values in the right superior frontal gyrus WM after controlling for age, sex, hypertension, and heart disease.	The small sample size and the cross-sectional study design are major limitations.	WM microstructure changes of the right superior frontal gyrus are associated with LLD.	Taylor *et al.* [48]
Cross-sectional open, but controlled, treatment	13 elderly patients with MDD	According to survival analysis with Cox's proportional hazards model, a	The preliminary nature of data together with the small sample size did not allow the	Microstructural WM abnormalities lateral to the anterior cingulate	Alexopoulos *et al.* [42]

Table 1: contd…

Study Design	Sample	Main Results	Limitations	Conclusion	Reference
with citalopram at 40 mg for 12 weeks		decreased FA of the right and left frontal WM regions 15 mm above the anterior commissure-posterior commissure plane has been associated with a lower remission rate even after controlling for age.	generalization of the present results. .	resulted associated with decreased rate of remission of geriatric depression.	

Note: AL=Activity levels; ACC=Anterior cingulate cortex; AD=Antidepressant; ADC=Apparent diffusion coefficient; ATR=Right anterior thalamic radiation; CES-D=Center for Epidemiologic Studies Depression Scale; CB=Cingulum bundle; CC=Corpus callosum; DSM-IV-TR=Diagnostic and Statistical Manual, IV Edition, Text Revision; DLPFC=Dorsolateral prefrontal cortex; DTI=Diffusion tensor imaging; EPI=Echo-planar imaging; FA=Fractional anisotropy; FC=Functional connectivity; GDS-15=Geriatric Depression Scale 15-item; HC=Healthy controls; LLD=Late-life depression; M1=Motor cortex (primary); MDD=Major Depressive Disorder; MD=Mean Diffusivity; MFB=Medial forebrain bundle; MINI=Mini-international neuropsychiatric interview; MTL=Medial temporal lobe; NNF=Normalized number of fibers; rACC=Rostral anterior cingulate cortex; RD=Radial diffusivity; ROI=Region-of-interest; RST=Right solitary tract; SLF=Superior longitudinal fasciculus; SMA=Supplementary motor area; TBSS=Tract-based spatial statistics; TOI=Tract of interest; UF=Uncinate fasciculus; VBA=Voxel-based analysis; VTA-dlPFC=Ventral tegmental area-dorsolateral prefrontal cortex; VTA-lOFC=Ventral tegmental area-lateral orbitofrontal cortex; Voxel-based analysis=VBA; WMH=White Matter Hyperintensity; WM=White matter.

The Effect of Treatments on WM Integrity

The majority of DTI studies about the effects of treatments on WM integrity have been previously discussed. However, Table **2** reports the most relevant DTI studies showing the positive effect of treatments on WM integrity in patients with MDD.

Table 2. DTI studies demonstrating the positive effect of treatments on WM integrity in patients with MDD.

Study Design	Sample	Main Results	Limitations	Conclusion	Reference
1 week follow-up study after completion of ECT series	20 MDD patients and 28 HC	Patients had higher FA values in dorsal fronto-limbic circuits encompassing the anterior cingulum, forceps minor, and left superior longitudinal fasciculus between baseline and transition to	Only ROI analyses showed significant diagnostic group effects that are subtle. Non-tensor models applied to diffusion data may better resolve differences in WM areas with crossing fibers.	MDD patients showed abnormal WM microstructure in fronto-limbic networks, modulated by ECT and related to therapeutic response. Increased FA and decreased MD	Lyden *et al.* [17]

Table 2: contd…

Study Design	Sample	Main Results	Limitations	Conclusion	Reference
		maintenance therapy. Lower RD and MD were also observed in overlapping regions and the anterior thalamic radiation. DTI metrics associated with therapeutic response in tracts showing significant ECT effects differed between MDD patients and HC. All measures remained stable across time in controls.		and RD suggest increased fiber integrity in dorsal fronto-limbic pathways involved in mood regulation and a trend towards normative values with treatment.	
Retrospective chart review study (Cross-sectional)	92 MDD patients (29 non remitters, 26 partial remitters, 37 full-remitters), and 58 HC	Failure to achieve remission was associated with lower FA among MDD patients, statistically significant for the medial body of the fornix. Global and regional-selective age-related FA decline was prominent in patients with treatment-refractory, non-remitted depression.	The cross-sectional data, imaging legacy data, and clinical characterization based on review of medical records were major limitations. Considering the large database available, larger final sample sizes may have been expected.	Specific brain microstructural WM abnormalities may be found underlying persistent, treatment-resistant depression.	Hoogenboom *et al.* [18]
Cross-sectional	134 MDD patients and 54 HC	When compared with HC, MDD patients demonstrated no significant differences in FA, RD, MD, and axonal diffusivity with either the VBM or the TBSS approach.	Findings are limited by the cross-sectional study design and the not full data on smoking status and hypertension is another limitation.	WM integrity could not play a critical role in the pathophysiology of MDD.	Choi *et al.* [19]
5 week follow-up after a four-week course of GI	21 MDD patients and 22 HC	MDD patients demonstrated a significant reduction in the HDRS-17 and	Major limitations are: small sample size, ages and illness durations not	When compared to HC, WM abnormalities have been	Wang *et al.* [30]

Table 2: contd…

Study Design	Sample	Main Results	Limitations	Conclusion	Reference
PT		higher FA in the right thalamus post-treatment. Psychopathological changes did not recover post-treatment but increased FA was reported in the frontal lobe.	completely homogeneous, the control group that was not rescanned after a similar 4 weeks interval; a PT-prone bias due to the enrolled MDD subjects voluntarily recruited GI therapy; neuropsychological testing was not carried out to further support the speculated behavioral and cognitive defects.	demonstrated within the sub-cortical, cortical, and cerebellum regions of MDD patients. Also, post-treatment effects showed an increase in FA within the left frontal lobe. These findings supported the proposed ‘‘top-down’’ mechanism of PT.	
Follow-up after a course of bilateral ECT	8 LLD patients and 12 age-matched HC	Before ECT treatment, significant FA decrease was found in several frontal and temporal brain regions in LLD patients compared to HC. A significant increase in frontal WM FA was observed after ECT. WM integrity in frontal brain regions improved after a course of bilateral ECT.	The small sample size did not allow the generalization of the present findings.	The present findings suggested a strong relationship between WM integrity and antidepressant action of ECT.	Nobuhara *et al.* [44]
12 week open-label trial	74 MDD older patiens	Not-remitted MDD patients showed higher FA values in the superior frontal gyri and anterior cingulate cortices bilaterally. Also, no statistically significant associations between ADC measures and remission were found.	The study lacked of covariates in statistical model and did not control for multiple comparisons. In addition, MRI data were obtained after start of sertraline treatment.	An association between failure to remit to sertraline and higher FA values in frontal lobe was reported. MDD is characterized by functional disconnection between frontal and limbic regions and subjects with structural disconnection	Taylor *et al.* [64]

Table 2: contd…

Study Design	Sample	Main Results	Limitations	Conclusion	Reference
				identified by DTI may be more likely to respond to antidepressants.	
RCT	8 patients with mild to moderately resistant MDD (4 active rTMS, 4 sham rTMS)	A mean increase was found for the LPF-WM. The mixed model suggested a trend toward a significant Treatment Group × Region interaction effect. Further, simple Region effects (left prefrontal WM *vs.* right prefrontal WM) were at a trend toward significance for difference after treatment within the active rTMS group but not within the sham rTMS group.	The small sample size is a major limitation.	rTMS resulted was not associated with damage of WM on the side of stimulation. DTI techniques may offer a unique modality to investigate mechanisms of action underlying rTMS.	Kozel *et al.* [65]
Cross-sectional	47 elderly depressed patients and 36 elderly HC	No significant differences among FA and MD parameters were observed among patients, even after control for age. Also, no significant correlations were found between cognitive performance and FA or MD.	Major limitations are: MRI examination; a group heterogeneity regarding education; MDD patients with mild to moderate depressive symptoms; lack of data concerning duration of disease and duration of the antidepressant therapy.	No significant differences among FA or MD values were observed between mildly or moderately depressed and non-depressed elderly patients when the brain was analyzed without a determined ROI.	Bezerra *et al.* [66]
Cross-sectional	21 right handed MDD patients and 42 age- and gender-matched right-handed HC	Compared to HC, MDD patients demostrated local regions of significant GM volume reduction in the right parahippocampal gyrus, hippocampus, bilateral middle frontal gyri, bilateral	Age at onset, time of examination, depression severity, drug doses, time since clinical remission and duration of medication could have contributed to the present findings. Also, the inclusion	Fronto-limbic neural circuit might show a critical role in the neurobiology of MDD.	Abe *et al.* [67]

Table 2: contd…

Study Design	Sample	Main Results	Limitations	Conclusion	Reference
		anterior cingulate cortices, left parietal and occipital lobes, and right superior temporal gyrus. Local regions showing an increase of MD in MDD patients were observed in the bilateral parahippocampal gyri, hippocampus, pons, cerebellum, left frontal and temporal lobes, and right frontal lobe. FA tended to correlate negatively with total days depressed in the right anterior cingulate and the WM of the left frontal lobe.	of patients with lower HDRS total scores might have determined the absence of a significant correlation between regional volume or diffusion properties and HDRS. Other limitations are: the low spatial and angular resolutions and voxel-based analyses that may tend to yield more false positive.		
Cross-sectional	16 MDD patients and 20 HC	MDD patients showed a trend for lower FA values in the left sagittal stratum suggesting decreased FA in the right cingulate cortex and posterior body of CC. After regression analyses, the lower FA in sagittal stratum regions disappeared.	Major limitations are: small sample size; cross-sectional study design; lack of analysis on the possible effects of medication.	MDD patients had reduced FA in the left sagittal stratum relative to controls. The study identified three fundamental WM tracts contribute to the limbic-cortical network and visual system region.	Kieseppä *et al.* [68]

Note: ADC=Apparent Diffusion Coefficient; CC=Corpus callosum; DTI=Diffusion tensor imaging; ECT=Electroconvulsive Treatment; FA=Fractional anisotropy; GI=Guided imagery; GM=Grey matter; HDRS-17=Hamilton Depression Rating Scale-17 items; HC=healthy controls; LPF-WM=Left prefrontal white matter; LLD=Late-life depression; MD=Mean diffusivity; MDD=Major Depressive Disorder; MRI=Magnetic Resonance Imaging; PT=Psychotherapy; RCT=Randomized controlled trial; rTMS=Repetitive Transcranial Magnetic Stimulation; ROI=Region of interest; RD=Radial diffusivity; TBSS=tract-based spatial statistics; VBM=Voxel-based morphometry; WM=White matter.

The Impact of Microstructural WM Brain Alterations as Assessed by DTI in Patients with Suicidal Behavior

The neurobiological mechanisms underlying suicidal behavior are largely unknown; however, the identification of WM abnormalities using tract-based spatial sequences has recently contributed to clarify the pathophysiology of suicidal behavior. Several studies analyzed this topic suggesting the existence of a neurobiological vulnerability for suicide related to WM microstructure. Olvet *et al.* [31] reported lower FA values in the dorsomedial prefrontal cortex (DMPFC) of 13 suicide attempters affected by MDD when compared with healthy controls and depressed patients who did not attempt suicide. Previously, a functional MRI study reported a reduced activation in the DMPFC of remitted MDD suicide attempters compared with controls who did not attempt suicide [69]. Some studies analyzing the integrity of WM microstructure in patients with a history of suicide attempts investigated samples of war veterans. Lopez-Larson *et al.* [32] found greater FA values in bilateral thalamic radiations, a negative correlation between right thalamic volume and anxiety symptoms and a positive correlation between right anterior thalamic radiations FA and impulsivity in veterans with mild traumatic brain injury and a history of suicidal behavior compared to healthy controls or veterans affected by mild traumatic brain injury but without history of suicidal behavior. Moreover, cingulate FA values have been positively related with current suicidal ideation in veterans [33].

Finally, the effect on WM microstructure of lifetime suicide attempts has also been investigated in subjects affected by MDD (who were attempters and non-attempters) compared to healthy controls [34]. Having a history of suicide attempts has been related to greater WM abnormalities in orbitofrontal cortex and thalamus. Conversely, both groups revealed a decrease in fibre projections through the ALIC to the left medial frontal cortex, orbitofrontal cortex and thalamus (for more details, see Table **2**).

Table 3. Most relevant studies about the association between WM abnormalities and affective temperaments in patients with MDD and suicidal behavior.

Study Design	Sample	Main Results	Limitations	Conclusion	References
Cross-sectional	100 healthy individuals	Cerebellar grey matter volumes and FA were associated positively NS scores as assessed by TCI, and negatively with grey matter MD.	The study included healthy subjects. Also, the potential causal link between cerebellar structures and novelty-related behaviors has	The cerebellum may play a key role in novelty-related behaviors.	Picerni *et al.* [70]

Table 3: contd…

Study Design	Sample	Main Results	Limitations	Conclusion	References
		Cerebellar structural measures resulted not associated with Harm Avoidance, Reward Dependence or Persistence scores.	not been measured. Finally, the cross-sectional nature of the study is another limitation.		
Cross-sectional	125 healthy adults	Higher NS scores were associated with increased bilateral caudate and pallidum volumes. Also, higher HA scores as assessed by TCI resulted associated with increased MD in the bilateral putamen. Macro/micro-structural variations in the basal ganglia regions may partially explain the biological variance associated with NS or HA personality phenotype.	First, the study included healthy subjects. Furthermore, the cross-sectional nature of the study is another limitation.	Subjects who have higher MD values throughout the micro-structure of putamen may be more vulnerable in experiencing negative symptoms, withdrawal, and inhibition.	Laricchiuta *et al.* [71]
Cross-sectional	263 healthy adults	Decreased FA in anterior regions including frontostriatal and frontolimbic circuits was associated with increased RD. Reduced microstructural integrity of the brain WM as showed by negative associations between RD and FA is associated with higher RD. The study did not support the association between NS and DTI indices.	First, the study included healthy individuals. Importantly, the cross-sectional nature of this study is a further limitation.	Variability in RD may be related to reduced WM integrity of frontostriatal and frontolimbic circuits.	Bjørnebekk *et al.* [72]
Cross-sectional	263 healthy adults	Decreased FA and increased MD and RD in WM corticolimbic tracts have been associated with increased HA.	The study included healthy individuals. Histological findings were not available. Importantly, the cross-sectional nature of this study is another additional limitation.	Anxiety-related aspects of personality may be affected by structural corticolimbic connectivity. A higher susceptibility to psychiatric	Westye *et al.* [73]

Table 3: contd…

Study Design	Sample	Main Results	Limitations	Conclusion	References
				disease may be reflected by reduced WM integrity.	
Cross-sectional	68 female volunteers	The study found a correlation between temperament traits evaluated by TCI and WM volume. In particular, a connection between cooperativeness and WM volume of the medial frontal and precentral gyrus has been suggested.	The study included healthy subjects and DTI techniques were not used. Environmental factors (potentially influencing personality traits) have been not controlled. Importantly, the cross-sectional nature of the study is another additional limitation.	Individual variations in brain morphology may be associated with temperament and character dimensions.	Van Schuerbeek *et al.* [74]
Cross-sectional	42 healthy aged adults	GM volume of the temporal, parietal, and frontal cortices, and self-transcendence (a personality trait presumably reflecting mature creativity and spiritualism) have been positively associated.	First, the study has been carried out on healthy subjects. Some associations were significant only after correction for age and sex. Also, the relatively small differences of cooperativeness scores in healthy subjects may have had little impact on behavior. Importantly, the cross-sectional nature of the study is another limitation.	The relatively greater temporal cortical GM volumes resulted associated with high self-transcendence having adaptive advantages in the later part of life.	Kaasinen *et al.* [75]
2-year follow-up	28 EOD elderly patients and 48 HP	Increased Neuroticism factor, Anxiety facet scores, and decreased Warmth and Positive Emotions facet scores were all found at baseline but reached the level of HP at follow-up. Also, significantly higher depression facet scores were reported in EOD patients than HP at both baseline and after 2 years independently of depressive relapse.	24% of the participants at follow-up. Also, the study did not consider a comparison with LOD patients.	The long-term assessment of MDD may be characterized by the trait like marker depression-related personality facet.	Weber *et al.* [76]

Table 3: contd…

Study Design	Sample	Main Results	Limitations	Conclusion	References
Cross-sectional	247 subjects with major affective disorders	The study reported that 48% of patients had periventricular WMHs and 39% deep WMHs. Patients with higher dysthymia and lower hyperthymia were more likely to have hopelessness, more WMHs, and more recent suicide attempts relative to patients with higher hyperthymia and lower dysthymia.	The association between the lethality/number of suicide attempts and the presence/ severity/number of hyperintensities has not been investigated. Finally, the lack of accounting for the cognitive effects of medications as well as the cross-sectional nature of the study are other shortcomings.	Differences in the subcortical structures of the brain are associated with different temperament profiles.	Serafini *et al.* [86]

Note: DTI=Diffusion tensor imaging; EOD=Early-onset depression; FA=Fractional anisotropy; GM=grey matter; HA=Harm Avoidance; HP=healthy participants; LOD=late-onset depression; MD=mean diffusivity; NS=Novelty seeking; RD=Reward dependence; TCI=Temperament and Character Inventory; WM=White matter; WMHs=White matter hyperintensities.

WM Alterations as Assessed by DTI and Temperaments: Implications Concerning MDD and Suicidality

The association between WM microstructural alterations and affective temperaments has been investigated in seven DTI studies. Macro- and micro-structural variations of cerebellum WM have been investigated with DTI in a group of healthy subjects and related to temperamental traits as assessed by Temperament and Character Inventory (TCI) [70]. The study revealed a positive correlation between higher FA values and higher novelty-seeking scores and suggested that posterior vermis WM tracts may play a central role in novelty-seeking behaviors. Laricchiuta *et al.* [71] have previously reported in a study on healthy subjects that the scores in the four temperamental scales of TCI were positively associated with the volumes of cerebellar WM.

Bjørnebekk and colleagues [72] investigated a possible association between WM abnormalities and social reward dependency using DTI technique in healthy individuals. Results showed lower FA values in subjects with higher reward dependence and suggested that WM of the anterior brain areas may modulate individual differences in social reward although no significant association was observed between novelty seeking behaviors and WM microstructure. In a large sample of healthy subjects, an increase in harm avoidance has been correlated with lower FA values and higher mean/radial diffusivity in those corticolimbic WM networks which are supposed to play a key role in emotional processing and reappraisal [73]. The study suggested the early onset of the associations between WM structure and anxiety-related personality traits and their tendency to emerge early in life and remain stable.

The relationship between temperaments and WM microstructure has also been analyzed by two voxel-based morphometry studies. In the first study, Van Schuerbeek *et al.* [74] investigated healthy female individuals and found a significant correlation between cooperativeness and medial frontal and precentral gyrus WM volumes. In addition, Kaasinen *et al.* [75] found no correlation between WM volumes and personality traits in older healthy subjects but only a trend between right cerebellar WM volume and self-transcendence.

Table **4** summarizes the most relevant studies about the association between WM microstructural features and affective temperaments in patients with major depression and suicidal behavior.

Table 4. Most relevant DTI studies about alterations in WM integrity and suicidal behavior.

Study Design	Sample	Main Results	Limitations	Conclusion	References
Cross-sectional	13 suicide attempters with MDD, 39 non-attempters with MDD, 46 HP	Lower FA relative to MDD non-attempters and HP in the DLPFC were found in suicide attempters. A significant cluster within the right DLPFC was also reported according to uncorrected TBSS findings.	First, the small sample size did not allow the generalization of findings. HP group was younger than the non-attempter group. Furthermore, the most recent suicide attempt ranged from 19 days to 39 years before the DTI scan. The possible effect of antidepressants who were taken by participants may be not excluded. Importantly, the cross-sectional nature of the study is another additional limitation.	Functional deficits in suicidal behavior may be at least partially related to WM abnormalities.	Olvet *et al.* [31]
Cross-sectional	40 Veterans with mild TBI and no SB, 19	Significantly increased left and right thalamic volumes were found in those with TBI	First, the small sample size. Furthermore, the study included only male subjects. Also, the cross-sectional	Individuals with TBI together with a history of SB had enlargement and increased FA	Lopez-Larson *et al.* [32]

Table 4: contd…

Study Design	Sample	Main Results	Limitations	Conclusion	References
	Veterans with mild TBI and a history of SB, 15 HP	and a history of SB relative to the HP, TBI and a history of SB, and the combined group. Veterans with TBI/a history of SB had increased FA bilaterally than HP, HP/ TBI and a history of SB group, TBI and a history of SB only group. Significant positive associations were reported for bilateral ATR and BIS in those with TBI and a history of SB.	nature of this study is another limitation.	throughout the thalamus that may be implicated as a potential biomarker of suicidal behavior.	
Cross-sectional	Fifteen male veterans with TBI, 17 matched HP	TBI subjects exhibited a significant reduction in FA values of the left cingulum and left/total genu relative to HP. Individuals with TBI were more likely to have higher impulsivity than HP. A positive correlation between current suicidal ideation, impulsivity, and total and right cingulum FA has been reported.	First, the small sample size did not allow the generalization of findings. In addition, the cross-sectional nature of the study is another relevant limitation.	A significant reduction in FA of frontal WM tracts in veterans with mild TBI associated with both impulsivity and suicidality may suggest the existence of a potential vulnerability to suicidal risk.	Yurgelun-Todd *et al.* [33]
Cross-sectional	63 patients with MDD (23 with and 40 without a history of suicide attempts), 46 HP	Decreased fibre projections through the ALIC to the left medial frontal cortex, orbitofrontal cortex and thalamus may be found in both groups of depressed subjects. More abnormalities throughout the left	Specific method of suicide attempts, specific previous treatments, or number of previous attempts and depressive episodes have been not analyzed. Also, personality has not been evaluated. Importantly, the	Cognitive/affective dysfunctions associated with vulnerability for suicidal behavior in depressed patients may be also related to WM alterations of frontothalamic circuits.	Jia *et al.* [34]

Table 4: contd…

Study Design	Sample	Main Results	Limitations	Conclusion	References
		orbitofrontal cortex and thalamus may be observed in those with a history of suicide attempts compared to those without suicide attempts.	ability to distinguish the directionality of altered fibre tracts is limited. Moreover, the degree to which alterations in the ALIC are restricted to the left hemisphere needs to be assessed. In summary, the present results are not able to ascertain the direction of causality.		

Note: ALIC= left anterior limb of the internal capsule; ATR=anterior thalamic radiations; BIS=Barratt Impulsiveness Scale; DTI=Diffusion tensor imaging; DLPFC=dorsolateral prefrontal cortex; FA=Fractional anisotropy; HP=healthy participants; MDD=Major depressive disorder; SB=suicidal behavior; TBI=traumatic brain injury; TBSS=tract-based spatial statistics; WM=white matter

DISCUSSION

Based on the main results of the present review chapter, DTI studies found a robust association between WM microstructural abnormalities, major depression and suicidal behavior. Studies reported that WM integrity abnormalities may be successfully investigated using DTI techniques in patients with MDD. According to the most relevant DTI evidence, alterations in WM integrity may be re-conceptualized as microstructural damage related to vascular processes in the context of brain connectivity [76].

Some mechanisms such as ischemia, micro infarcts [77, 78], cerebral edema [79], demyelination [80], astrocyte proliferation and deposition of brain toxic materials [80] have been hypothesized in the development of WM alterations. DTI techniques are able to detect important features of WM lesions such as location, orientation and anisotropy of the brain tracts. Considering that WM alterations may be associated with poor clinical course, disability, psychosocial impairment, [81] poor response to treatment and functional decline [82-85], clinicians should deeply understand the nature and origin of WM alterations in MDD. WM microstructure alterations as investigated by DTI techniques may show several aspects underlying the pathophysiology of MDD with and without suicidal behavior (Tables **1-3**).

Importantly, neuroimaging findings are also able to increase our understanding about the complex association between affective temperaments, personality profiles and WM microstructural alterations (Table **4**). As suggested by Serafini *et al.* [86], dysthymic temperamental traits together with deep brain abnormalities may significantly predict a negative outcome, triggering suicidality in patients with MDD. Clinicians could screen patients for the presence of WM abnormalities and dysthymic temperament profile for identifying a subgroup of MDD patients with higher disability and more negative outcome than others and this may be useful to plan the best treatment strategy. The association between microstructural WM abnormalities, major depression and suicidality may be further confirmed by the earlier age at onset of illness in some subgroups of patients with MDD, higher WM abnormalities and the increased suicidality in those patients with early-onset mood disorders compared with other subgroups [2].

In 1964, Hopkinson [87] found for the first time that first-degree relatives of depressed subjects were more likely to be at risk of depression (20%) in the early-onset depression group compared with the late-onset depression group (8.3%). Similarly, Schultz [88] and Post [89] replicated these results suggesting that genetic factors may exert greater effects in subjects with early-onset depression than in those with late-onset depression. More than thirty years later, Takahashi and colleagues [90] validated the general assumption that early-onset type may be more closely associated with non-vascular (*e.g.*, genetic) factors.

Furthermore, WM lesions have been found significantly associated with age at initial onset of depression (45.8 years) by Komaki and colleagues [91] in MDD subjects. Interestingly, patients with lacunar infarction were reported at significantly higher rate of suicide compared with subjects with no abnormal findings or WMHs, but no lacunar infarction. It has been hypothesized that general outcomes in those with lacunar infarction were poorer compared with the other two groups. However, it's also important to state that a direct correlation between subcortical hyperintensities and age at onset in individuals with major affective disorders was not reported in all studies [92-94].

Alterations of WM integrity may be related to multiple (*e.g.*, progressive or rather static) factors occurring in younger adults without apparent medical conditions or may be genetically determined in those with inflammatory/demyelinating diseases [95]. WM integrity has been recently reported as an interesting endophenotype for bipolar disorder with important behavioral associations linked to the etiology of this condition by Sprooten *et al.* [96]. The authors found the existence of a reduction in WM integrity when analyzing unaffected relatives of bipolar patients and cyclothymic temperament. Impaired WM integrity has been proposed as one of the possible mechanisms of genetic predisposition underlying bipolar disorder although patients with a history of suicide and implications related to suicide risk have not been investigated in the mentioned study. In addition, mood instability has been linked to reduced fronto-temporal and fronto-thalamic WM integrity in healthy control subjects as well as unaffected relatives at high genetic risk for bipolar disorder. In addition, WM integrity of the internal capsules bilaterally and left temporal lobe was negatively associated with cyclothymia in high-risk subjects together with controls.

The following limitations that did not allow the generalization of the present findings should be adequately taken into account. First, although DTI techniques permitted to detect and investigate microstructural dysfunctions affecting brain connectivity, the exact nature of these alterations is still poorly understood. In addition, there are studies in literature that did not select patients for the presence/severity of confounding factors such as age, vascular risk factors, history of substance abuse/dependence, number and severity of previous mood episodes and comorbid conditions. Notably, the use of psychotropic medications in the patients which were included may also potentially influence both the presence and severity of WM lesions.

CONCLUSION

It has been suggested that WM is not a passive tissue but it is actively implicated in major psychiatric conditions. Fundamental human abilities such as affect, learning, memory and self-control ability may be affected by the timing of WM growth and degree of completion.

We suggest that WM abnormalities in patients with MDD may be possible biological markers of poor outcome and they can also trigger suicidal behavior. The presence of WM alterations may be also identified as a predictor of illness severity and psychosocial impairment.

However, additional longitudinal studies are required in order to promptly identify those patients with a lower psychosocial functioning and more negative outcomes in the effort to clarify the biological processes involved underlying the progression of WM alterations in major affective disorders.

CONFLICT OF INTERESTS

The authors confirm that the present chapter contents have no conflict of interest.

ACKNOWLEDGEMENTS

Declared none.

REFERENCES

[1] Cho DY, Lee WY, Chen CC. Limbic leukotomy for intractable major affective disorders: a 7-year follow-up study using nine comprehensive psychiatric test evaluations. J Clin Neurosci 2008; 15: 138-42.
[2] Rihmer Z. Suicide risk in mood disorders. Curr Opin Psychiatry 2007; 20: 17-22.
[3] Hawton K, van Heeringen K. Suicide. Lancet 2009; 373: 1372-81.
[4] Thomas AJ, Perry R, Barber R, Kalaria RN, O'Brien JT. Pathologies and pathological mechanisms for white matter hyperintensities in depression. Ann NY Acad Sci 2002; 977: 333-9.
[5] Thomas AJ, O'Brien JT, Davis S, *et al.* Ischemic basis for deep white matter hyperintensities in major depression: a neuropathological study. Arch Gen Psychiatry 2002; 59: 785-92.
[6] Ehrlich S, Noam GG, Lyoo IK, Kwon BJ, Clark MA, Renshaw PF. Subanalysis of the location of white matter hyperintensities and their association with suicidality in children and youth. Ann N Y Acad Sci 2003; 1008: 265-8.
[7] Ehrlich S, Noam GG, Lyoo IK, Kwon BJ, Clark MA, Renshaw PF. White matter hyperintensities and their associations with suicidality in psychiatrically hospitalized children and adolescents. J Am Acad Child Adolesc Psychiatry 2004; 43: 770-6.
[8] Ehrlich S, Breeze JL, Hesdorffer DC, *et al.* White matter hyperintensities and their association with suicidality in depressed young adults. J Affect Disord 2005; 86: 281-7.
[9] Pompili M, Ehrlich S, De Pisa E, *et al.* White matter hyperintensities and their associations with suicidality in patients with major affective disorders. Eur Arch Psychiatry Clin Neurosci 2007; 257: 494-9.
[10] Zanetti MV, Schaufelberger MS, de Castro CC, *et al.* White-matter hyperintensities in first-episode psychosis. Br J Psychiatry 2008; 193: 25-30.
[11] Qin J, Wei M, Liu H, *et al.* Abnormal hubs of white matter networks in the frontal-parieto circuit contribute to depression discrimination *via* pattern classification. Magn Reson Imaging 2014; pii: S0730-725X(14)00268-9.
[12] Lai CH, Wu YT. Alterations in white matter micro-integrity of the superior longitudinal fasciculus and anterior thalamic radiation of young adult patients with depression. Psychol Med 2014; 44: 2825-32.
[13] LeWinn KZ, Connolly CG, *et al.* White matter correlates of adolescent depression: structural evidence for frontolimbic disconnectivity. J Am Acad Child Adolesc Psychiatry 2014; 53: 899-909, 909.e1-7.
[14] Korgaonkar MS, Williams LM, Song YJ, Usherwood T, Grieve SM. Diffusion tensor imaging predictors of treatment outcomes in major depressive disorder. Br J Psychiatry 2014a; 205: 321-8.
[15] Korgaonkar MS, Fornito A, Williams LM, Grieve SM. Abnormal structural networks characterize major depressive disorder: a connectome analysis. Biol Psychiatry 2014b; 76: 567-74.
[16] Song YJ, Korgaonkar MS, Armstrong LV, Eagles S, Williams LM, Grieve SM. Tractography of the brainstem in major depressive disorder using diffusion tensor imaging. PLoS One 2014; 9: e84825
[17] Lyden H, Espinoza RT, Pirnia T, *et al.* Electroconvulsive therapy mediates neuroplasticity of white matter microstructure in major depression. Transl Psychiatry 2014; 4: e380.
[18] Hoogenboom WS, Perlis RH, Smoller JW, *et al.* Limbic system white matter microstructure and long-term treatment outcome in major depressive disorder: a diffusion tensor imaging study using legacy data. World J Biol Psychiatry 2014; 15: 122-34.
[19] Choi KS, Holtzheimer PE, Franco AR, *et al.* Reconciling variable findings of white matter integrity in major depressive disorder. Neuropsychopharmacology 2014; 39: 1332-9.
[20] de Kwaasteniet B, Ruhe E, Caan M, *et al.* Relation between structural and functional connectivity in major depressive disorder. Biol Psychiatry 2013; 74: 40-7.

[21] Macmaster FP, Carrey N, Marie Langevin L. Corpus callosal morphology in early onset adolescent depression. J Affect Disord 2013; 145: 256-9.

[22] Hayakawa YK, Sasaki H, Takao H, *et al.* Structural brain abnormalities in women with subclinical depression, as revealed by voxel-based morphometry and diffusion tensor imaging. J Affect Disord 2013; 144: 263-8.

[23] Henderson SE, Johnson AR, Vallejo AI, Katz L, Wong E, Gabbay V. A preliminary study of white matter in adolescent depression: relationships with illness severity, anhedonia, and irritability. Front Psychiatry 2013; 4: 152.

[24] Bessette KL, Nave AM, Caprihan A, Stevens MC. White matter abnormalities in adolescents with major depressive disorder. Brain Imaging Behav 2014; 8: 531-41.

[25] Tha KK, Terae S, Nakagawa S, *et al.* Impaired integrity of the brain parenchyma in non-geriatric patients with major depressive disorder revealed by diffusion tensor imaging. Psychiatry Res 2013; 212: 208-15.

[26] Bracht T, Horn H, Strik W, *et al.* White matter microstructure alterations of the medial forebrain bundle in melancholic depression. J Affect Disord 2014; 155: 186-93.

[27] Bracht T, Federspiel A, Schnell S, *et al.* Cortico-cortical white matter motor pathway microstructure is related to psychomotor retardation in major depressive disorder. PLoS One 2012; 7: e52238.

[28] Osoba A, Hänggi J, Li M, *et al.* Disease severity is correlated to tract specific changes of fractional anisotropy in MD and CM thalamus--a DTI study in major depressive disorder. J Affect Disord 2013; 149: 116-28.

[29] Liao Y, Huang X, Wu Q, *et al.* Is depression a disconnection syndrome? Meta-analysis of diffusion tensor imaging studies in patients Muwith MDD. J Psychiatry Neurosci 2013; 38: 49-56.

[30] Wang T, Huang X, Huang P, *et al.* Early-stage psychotherapy produces elevated frontal white matter integrity in adult major depressive disorder. PLoS One 2013; 8: e63081.

[31] Olvet DM, Peruzzo D, Thapa-Chhetry B, *et al.* A diffusion tensor imaging study of suicide attempters. J Psychiatr Res 2014; 51: 60-7.

[32] Lopez-Larson M, King JB, McGlade E, *et al.* Enlarged thalamic volumes and increased fractional anisotropy in the thalamic radiations in veterans with suicide behaviors. Front Psychiatry 2013; 4: 83.

[33] Yurgelun-Todd DA, Bueler CE, McGlade EC, Churchwell JC, Brenner LA, Lopez-Larson MP. Neuroimaging correlates of traumatic brain injury and suicidal behavior. J Head Trauma Rehabil 2011; 26: 276-89.

[34] Jia Z, Wang Y, Huang X, *et al.* Impaired frontothalamic circuitry in suicidal patients with depression revealed by diffusion tensor imaging at 3.0 T. J Psychiatry Neurosci 2014; 39: 170-7.

[35] Taylor WD, Payne ME, Krishnan KR, *et al.* Evidence of white matter tract disruption in MRI hyperintensities. Biol. Psychiatry 2001; 50; 179-83.

[36] Soares JC, Mann JJ. The anatomy of mood disorders—review of structural neuroimaging studies. Biol Psychiatry 1997; 41: 86-106.

[37] Akiskal HS, Akiskal KK. TEMPS: Temperament Evaluation of Memphis, Pisa, Paris and San Diego. J Affect Disord 2005; 85: 1-2.

[38] Rihmer Z, Akiskal KK, Rihmer A, Akiskal HS. Current research on affective temperaments. Curr Opin Psychiatry 2010; 23: 12-8.

[39] Oedegaard KJ, Syrstad VE, Morken G, Akiskal HS, Fasmer OB. A study of age at onset and affective temperaments in a Norwegian sample of patients with mood disorders. J Affect Disord 2009; 118: 229-233.

[40] Parker G. Modern diagnostic concepts of the affective disorders. Acta Psychiatr Scand 2003; 24-8.

[41] Akiskal HS, Mallya G. Criteria for the "soft" bipolar spectrum: treatment implications. Psychopharmacol Bull 1987; 23: 68-73.

[42] Alexopoulos GS, Kiosses DN, Choi SJ, Murphy CF, Lim KO. Frontal white matter microstructure and treatment response of late-life depression: a preliminary study. Am J Psychiatry 2002; 159: 1929-32.

[43] Li L, Ma N, Li Z, *et al.* Prefrontal white matter abnormalities in young adult with major depressive disorder: a diffusion tensor imaging study. Brain Res 2007; 1168: 124-8.

[44] Ma N, Li L, Shu N, *et al.* White matter abnormalities in first-episode, treatment-naive young adults with major depressive disorder. Am J Psychiatry 2007; 164: 823-6.

[45] Walther S, Hügli S, Höfle O, *et al.* Frontal white matter integrity is related to psychomotor retardation in major depression. Neurobiol Dis 2012; 47: 13-9.

[46] Ouyang X, Tao HJ, Liu HH, *et al.* White matter integrity deficit in treatment-naïve adult patients with major depressive disorder. East Asian Arch Psychiatry 2011; 21: 5-9.

[47] Lamar M, Charlton RA, Morris RG, Markus HS. The impact of subcortical white matter disease on mood in euthymic older adults: a diffusion tensor imaging study. Am J Geriatr Psychiatry 2010; 18: 634-42.

[48] Taylor WD, MacFall JR, Payne ME, *et al.* Late-life depression and microstructural abnormalities in dorsolateral prefrontal cortex white matter. Am J Psychiatry 2004; 16: 1293-6.

[49] Nobuhara K, Okugawa G, Sugimoto T, *et al.* Frontal white matter anisotropy and symptom severity of late-life depression: a magnetic resonance diffusion tensor imaging study. J Neurol Neurosurg Psychiatry 2006; 77: 120-2.

[50] Kozel FA, Johnson KA, Nahas Z, *et al.* Fractional anisotropy changes after several weeks of daily left high-frequency repetitive transcranial magnetic stimulation of the prefrontal cortex to treat major depression. J ECT 2011; 27: 5-10.

[51] Zhu X, Wang X, Xiao J, Zhong M, Liao J, Yao S. Altered white matter integrity in first-episode, treatment-naive young adults with major depressive disorder: a tract-based spatial statistics study. Brain Res 2011; 1369: 223-9.

[52] Zou K, Huang X, Li T, *et al.* Alterations of white matter integrity in adults with major depressive disorder: a magnetic resonance imaging study. J Psychiatry Neurosci 2008; 33: 525-30.

[53] Alexopoulos GS, Murphy CF, Gunning-Dixon FM, *et al.* Microstructural white matter abnormalities and remission of geriatric depression. Am J Psychiatry. 2008; 165: 238-44.

[54] Murphy ML, Frodl T. Meta-analysis of diffusion tensor imaging studies shows altered fractional anisotropy occurring in distinct brain areas in association with depression. Biol Mood Anxiety Disord 2011; 1-3.

[55] Guo WB, Liu F, Xue ZM, *et al.* Altered white matter integrity in young adults with first-episode, treatment-naive, and treatment-responsive depression. Neurosci Lett 2012; 522: 139-44.

[56] Cullen KR, Klimes-Dougan B, Muetzel R, *et al.* Altered white matter microstructure in adolescents with major depression: a preliminary study. J Am Acad Child Adolesc Psychiatry 2010; 49: 173-83.e1.

[57] Korgaonkar MS, Grieve SM, Koslow SH, Gabrieli JD, Gordon E, Williams LM. Loss of white matter integrity in major depressive disorder: evidence using tract-based spatial statistical analysis of diffusion tensor imaging. Hum Brain Mapp 2011; 32: 2161-71.

[58] Colloby SJ, Firbank MJ, Thomas AJ, Vasudev A, Parry SW, O'Brien JT. White matter changes in late-life depression: a diffusion tensor imaging study. J Affect Disord 2011; 135: 216-20.

[59] Taylor WD, Kuchibhatla M, Payne ME, *et al.* Frontal white matter anisotropy and antidepressant remission in late-life depression. PLoS One 2008; 3: e3267.

[60] Wu F, Tang Y, Xu K, *et al.* Whiter matter abnormalities in medication-naive subjects with a single short-duration episode of major depressive disorder. Psychiatry Res 2011; 191: 80-3.

[61] Zhang A, Leow A, Ajilore O, *et al.* Quantitative tract-specific measures of uncinate and cingulum in major depression using diffusion tensor imaging. Neuropsychopharma-cology 2012; 37: 959-67.

[62] Aghajani M, Veer IM, van Lang ND, *et al.* Altered white-matter architecture in treatment-naive adolescents with clinical depression. Psychol Med 2013: 1-12.

[63] Cole J, Chaddock CA, Farmer AE, *et al.* White matter abnormalities and illness severity in major depressive disorder. Br J Psychiatry 2012; 201: 33-9.

[64] Bezerra DM, Pereira FR, Cendes F, *et al.* DTI voxelwise analysis did not differentiate older depressed patients from older subjects without depression. J Psychiatr Res 2012; 46: 1643-9.

[65] Abe O, Yamasue H, Kasai K, *et al.* Voxel-based analyses of gray/white matter volume and diffusion tensor data in major depression. Psychiatry Res 2010; 181: 64-70.

[66] Kieseppä T, Eerola M, Mäntylä R, *et al.* Major depressive disorder and white matter abnormalities: a diffusion tensor imaging study with tract-based spatial statistics. J Affect Disord 2010; 120: 240-4.

[67] Steffens DC, Taylor WD, Denny KL, Bergman SR, Wang L. Structural integrity of the uncinate fasciculus and resting state functional connectivity of the ventral prefrontal cortex in late life depression. PLoS One 2011; 6: e22697.

[68] Bae JN, MacFall JR, Krishnan KR, Payne ME, Steffens DC, Taylor WD. Dorsolateral prefrontal cortex and anterior cingulate cortex white matter alterations in late-life depression. Biol Psychiatry 2006; 60: 1356-63.
[69] Jollant F, Lawrence NS, Giampietro V, *et al.* Orbitofrontal cortex response to angry faces in men with histories of suicide attempts. Am J Psychiatry 2008; 165: 740-8.
[70] Picerni E, Petrosini L, Piras F, *et al.* New evidence for the cerebellar involvement in personality traits. Front Behav Neurosci 2013; 7: 133.
[71] Laricchiuta D, Petrosini L, Piras F, *et al.* Linking novelty seeking and harm avoidance personality traits to cerebellar volumes. Hum Brain Mapp 2014; 35: 285-96.
[72] Bjørnebekk A, Westlye LT, Fjell AM, Grydeland H, Walhovd KB. Social reward dependence and brain white matter microstructure. Cereb Cortex 2012; 22: 2672-9.
[73] Westlye LT, Bjørnebekk A, Grydeland H, Fjell AM, Walhovd KB. Linking an anxiety-related personality trait to brain white matter microstructure: diffusion tensor imaging and harm avoidance. Arch Gen Psychiatry 2011; 68: 369-77.
[74] Van Schuerbeek P, Baeken C, De Raedt R, De Mey J, Luypaert R. Individual differences in local gray and white matter volumes reflect differences in temperament and character: a voxel-based morphometry study in healthy young females. Brain Res 2011; 1371: 32-42.
[75] Kaasinen V, Maguire RP, Kurki T, Brück A, Rinne JO. Mapping brain structure and personality in late adulthood. Neuroimage 2005; 24: 315-22.
[76] Weber K, Giannakopoulos P, Delaloye C, *et al.* Personality traits, cognition and volumetric MRI changes in elderly patients with early-onset depression: a 2-year follow-up study. Psychiatry Res 2012; 198: 47-52.
[77] Krishnan KR, McDonald WM. Arteriosclerotic depression. Med Hypotheses 1995; 44: 111-5.
[78] Alexopoulos GS, Meyers BS, Young RC, Campbell S, Silbersweig D, Charlson M. 'Vascular depression' hypothesis. Arch Gen Psychiatry 1997; 54: 915-22.
[79] Lenze E, Cross D, McKeel D, Neuman RJ, Sheline YI. White matter hyperintensities and gray matter lesions in physically healthy depressed subjects. Am J Psychiatry 1999; 156: 1602-7.
[80] Thomas AJ, O'Brien JT, Davis S, *et al.* Ischemic basis for deep white matter hyperintensities in major depression: a neuropathological study. Arch Gen Psychiatry 2002c; 59: 785-92.
[81] Inzitari D, Simoni M, Pracucci G, *et al.* Risk of rapid global functional decline in elderly patients with severe cerebral age-related white matter changes: the LADIS study. Arch Intern Med 2007; 167: 81-88.
[82] Steffens DC, Bosworth HB, Provenzale JM, MacFall JR. Subcortical white matter lesions and functional impairment in geriatric depression. Depr Anxiety 2002; 15: 23-28.
[83] Steffens DC, Potter GG, McQuoid DR, *et al.* Longitudinal magnetic resonance imaging vascular changes, apolipoprotein E genotype, and development of dementia in the neurocognitive outcomes of depression in the elderly study. Am J Geriatr Psychiatry 2007; 15: 839-49.
[84] Teodorczuk A, O'Brien JT, Firbank MJ, *et al.* White matter changes and late-life depressive symptoms: longitudinal study. Br J Psychiatry 2007; 191: 212-7.
[85] Teodorczuk A, Firbank MJ, Pantoni L, *et al.* Relationship between baseline white-matter changes and development of late-life depressive symptoms: 3-year results from the LADIS study. Psychol Med 2010; 40: 603-10.
[86] Serafini G, Pompili M, Innamorati M, *et al.* Affective temperamental profiles are associated with white matter hyperintensity and suicidal risk in patients with mood disorders. J Affect Disord 2011; 129: 47-55.
[87] Hopkinson G. A genetic study of affective illness in patients over 50. Br J Psychiatry 1964; 110: 244-54.
[88] Schultz B. Auszalunger in der Verwandtschaft von nach Erkrankungsalter und Geschlechtgrupierten Manisch-Depressiven. Archiv fur Psychiatrie und Nervenkrankheiten 1951; 186: 560-76.
[89] Post F. Dementia depression and pseudodementia. In: Benson DF, Blumer D, Eds. Psychiatric aspects of neurologic disease. New York, Grune & Stratton, 1975.
[90] Takahashi K, Oshima A, Ida I, *et al.* Relationship between age at onset and magnetic resonance image-defined hyperintensities in mood disorders. J Psychiatr Res 2008; 42: 443-50.

[91] Komaki S, Nagayama H, Ohgami H, Takaki H, Mori H, Akiyoshi J. Prospective study of major depressive disorder with white matter hyperintensity: comparison of patients with and without lacunar infarction. Eur Arch Psychiatry Clin Neurosci 2008; 258: 160-4.

[92] Dupont RM, Jernigan TL, Butters N. Subcortical abnormalities detected in bipolar affective disorder using magnetic resonance imaging: clinical and neuropsychological significance. Arch Gen Psychiatry 1990; 47: 55-9.

[93] Figiel GS, Krishnan KRR, Rao VP, *et al.* Subcortical hyperintensities on brain magnetic resonance imaging: a comparison of normal and bipolar subjects. J Neuropsychiatry Clin Neurosci 1991; 3: 18-22.

[94] McDonald WM, Tupler LA, Marsteller FA, *et al.* Hyperintense lesions on magnetic resonance images in bipolar disorder. Biol Psychiatry 1999; 45: 965-71.

[95] Ringelstein EB, Kleffner I, Dittrich R, Kuhlenbaeumer G, Ritter MA. Hereditary and non-hereditary microangiopathies in the young. An up-date. J Neurol Sci 2010; 299: 81-5.

[96] Sprooten E, Sussmann JE, Clugston A, *et al.* White matter integrity in individuals at high genetic risk of bipolar disorder. Biol Psychiatry 2011; 70: 350-6.

Subject Index

Subject Index

A

B

C

Puneetpal Singh and Sarabjit Mastana (Eds)

D

E

F

N

O

P

W

www.ingramcontent.com/pod-product-compliance
Lightning Source LLC
LaVergne TN
LVHW070953210926
848482LV00002B/203